BABYLON

THE RESURGENCE OF HISTORY'S MOST INFAMOUS CITY

PETER HERDER
WITH BENJI NOLOT

forerunner
PUBLISHING

forerunner PUBLISHING

BABYLON: The Resurgence of History's Most Infamous City
By Peter Herder with Benji Nolot

Published by Forerunner Publishing
International House of Prayer
3535 E. Red Bridge Road
Kansas City, MO 64137
forerunnerpublishing@ihop.org
IHOP.org

ISBN 13: 978-0-9823262-0-6
ISBN 10: 0-9823262-0-3

Cover design by Seth Parks
Interior design by Dale Jimmo
Printed in the United States of America

TABLE OF CONTENTS

FOREWORD

WHEN PETER FIRST APPROACHED ME about working with him on this book, I immediately recognized the opportunity to advance the fight against slavery. Leading Exodus Cry has highlighted to me the need for a book that addresses the comprehensive historical and theological reasons for the emergence of human slavery in our day.

My involvement in this book has transformed my understanding of the prevalent social issues facing our world and reinvigorated me in the fight against slavery. As the director of Exodus Cry, an international anti-trafficking organization, I cannot imagine continuing on in this fight without a clear grasp of the underlying issues that this book develops. I am so grateful to Peter for the extensive and diligent labor he has invested in wading through the confusion around the mystery of Babylon and bringing to life the biblical vision of the world's most infamous city. It has been an unspeakable honor to join him in developing this subject at such a critical time.

In my work with Exodus Cry, I am daily confronted with the horrors of a world ravaged by the degradation of women and children. As I peer out across the landscape of the nations, I see a world whose moral fabric has been torn to shreds with the wholesale erosion of biblical values. This is not without consequence. An unprecedented movement of slavery and sexual exploitation is rising in the vacuum of moral decay.

As we examine the emergence of Babylon throughout history, it becomes clear that we must see the increase of human trafficking as the tip of a much larger historic iceberg. The nations are like passengers of a ship, unwittingly approaching their doom. The fog is lifting to expose the tip of an enormous danger visibly looming on the horizon. What is above the surface is only the beginning. Below the water lies a massive iceberg, lethal and unseen.

Modern-day slavery is one of several troubling trends that will converge in the birth of the next world empire: harlot Babylon. This book reveals not only visible trends like slavery and globalization, but also what lies below the surface. Reaching beyond issues of social justice, the contents of this book impinge upon every believer living in the end times. It is crucial for those alive today to not only grasp the malevolent events of the past, but also to connect the thread of darkness that is preparing the earth for the final Babylon.

Benji Nolot
Founder of Exodus Cry

INTRODUCTION

A MESSAGE FROM THE FUTURE

IMAGINE GOD SENT YOU BACK through time to the year 1928 with a divine mandate to prepare the Church for the coming decades. What would your message be? Just consider this question for a moment. Would you warn them the stock market would soon crash, leaving multitudes penniless? Or would you tell them to prepare for great difficulty because the days were coming when many would lose their employment and end up standing in bread lines?

To truly prepare the Church for what was coming, your message would have had to encompass far more than the imminent economic depression. The greatest threat on the horizon at that time was not financial. Over the course of the ensuing decades, the world would be forever changed. The Great Depression would open the door to an evil ideology that would drive the nations into global conflict. Millions of people would be systematically exterminated in a genocidal blood bath that would come to be known as the Holocaust. Millions of others would die in the Second World War. The Church would become divided and most believers would be criminally silent during the fateful years of Adolf Hitler's rise to power. Nations would be swept away in the propaganda of National Socialism. To the generation living in 1928, the imminent danger of the moment was the stock market crash that spawned the Great Depression, but the ultimate, and far greater threat, was Hitler's vision for a new world.

The day in which we live is not entirely unlike the days before the Great Depression. Once again we stand on the precipice of history. Behind us lies unprecedented prosperity. Before us lies great uncertainty. And just as in 1928, financial crisis and economic hardship are not the greatest threat we face. The great danger that lies before us is the emerging Antichrist system knocking at the door of history.

Now imagine God sent you forward through time a mere hundred years later. Once again the world is nothing like it is today. The years following the collapse of the US financial system have given birth to the greatest consolidation of power in history.

The United States has long since lost its status as the world's foremost economic power. Once the world's reserve currency, the US dollar has been replaced by a global e-currency. Trade barriers no longer exist. The one-world financial system is regulated by a central Bank of the World. Monetary policy, interest rates, and financing are controlled by a supreme central power.

A transition to this one-world financial system could only be accomplished through tremendous upheaval. Consolidating a global political authority became necessary for its full integration. Painful years of international conflict, social unrest, and a grassroots cry for peace became the birth canal of global government. In the final chapter of human history, the world has come under the control of a single governing body. National sovereignty is a relic of the past and a global senate now governs the nations of the earth. The world is no longer made up of nation-states but a series of regions, each with its representative senator. The policies and laws of the global senate are imposed upon all. Local government is a seamless extension of the universal headmaster. The US Constitution and Bill of Rights have been deserted except by a remnant of resisters.

Imagine a time where, around the world, there is no separation between state and religion—a time when the foremost spiritual leaders from around the globe have joined together to form a conglomeration of the world's religions. A one-world religion has been developed to unify the world. Its greatest objective is to celebrate and advance the unity and progression of the human race. It is the essence of humanism in its most virulent form. Religious extremists are targeted as the greatest threat to the international cooperation upon which the world government now depends. Polarizing religious views have been strictly forbidden. Universal spiritual pluralism is now the official religion of the state.

Welcome to the future, when human slavery, once a relic of the past, has become the most lucrative commercial enterprise in the world. Humans are bought, sold, and traded on an open market. At one time, human trafficking was a criminal engagement conducted on the black market. But now slavery has become a fully sanctioned commercial venture.

Just a couple of decades into the future, the world has been completely transformed under the influence of history's new world capital. A single city has risen to become the symbol of the pinnacle of human progress and glory. Replete with state-of-the-art architecture, it is the headquarters of the new world order. This city is the epicenter of the greatest consolidation of political, economic, and religious power in history. The global senate resides here. It is the home of the global stock exchange. And its central feature is the great temple tower of the one-world religion.

You might think this scenario is something out of a science fiction novel. In fact, it is taken from the Bible. While the timing of these events is uncertain, what is certain is that earth's future looks vastly different from our world today, and the birth pangs of the coming transition will soon seize the planet.

Endgame

We are experiencing the beginning of Satan's final attempt to seduce the nations with false promises of progress and glory; his ultimate agenda is global enslavement. Most are totally unaware of the magnitude of coming events and the corresponding upheaval that will transpire. A global currency is being prepared by the elite of the world's financial oligarchy. In many nations, political leaders are guiding their countries down a path to surrendering national sovereignty—a path leading to a global system with international regulations that will supersede our national boundaries. Prominent celebrities and religious leaders around the world are endorsing interfaith cooperation. The writing is on the wall; we are on the verge of global transition.

The reason these events are coming to pass can be summed up in one word: "Babylon." To understand why we are undergoing such great difficulty, we must understand what the Bible means by the word "Babylon." More than the headquarters of a global economic, political, and religious system, it is the key to Satan's end-time strategy to bring the nations under the power of the Antichrist.

In essence, this book is an unapologetic endeavor to understand what the Bible teaches about Babylon. It intends to fully lay bare the plan of Satan and understand our place in history, so that we can, without fear or confusion, fully and confidently participate in God's redemptive plan for the nations to glorify His name and usher in the coming of Jesus Christ.

To do this, we must start at the beginning, the Tower of Babel. We will go back to a time when the human race rebelled against the Creator to pursue the glory of human achievement. The fictional account that follows will provide context for the remainder of this book. Looking back into the dawn of history will give us a striking blueprint to understand the end of days. Woven into the untold story of the Tower of Babel is a historical pattern that is once again emerging in our day.

Next, we will unfold the theology behind Babylon to understand God's purposes and Satan's strategies. From there, we will venture through the Babylonian and Roman Empires. Finally, we will study how trends and events occurring today are paving the way for the future world capital.

If we want to understand why we are facing a historic crisis, we must understand and engage with what the Bible teaches about the unfolding story of Babylon. The Bible is the tale of two cities, Jerusalem and Babylon. This unfolding saga has everything to do with you, your future, and the choices you will have to make in the days that lie ahead. Discover your part of history.

PROLOGUE

THE TOWER OF BABEL
A FICTIONAL ACCOUNT

NOAH

NOAH AND HIS SONS STOOD upon the mountain, trembling before the Holy One. It was over, and it was just beginning. The endless days of darkness had ended. The relentless pounding of rain, driving winds, and waves had drowned out the memory of the violent years before the judgment fell. Now incense was rising to God on an altar of dry stones built by Noah's sons. It almost seemed like Eden again. Returning from the brink of annihilation, mankind had been reborn. They stood in awe as the glory of the Lord enveloped them.

> Be fruitful and multiply; teem on the earth and
> multiply in it.
>
> —Genesis 9:7

Noah's sons could hardly believe it. God was placing the entire span of His restored creation into their hands. They had witnessed the unrestrained tide of evil passions flooding the human family. But now a new dawn rose before them, cleansed from the defilement of bloodshed.

They were destined to become fathers of the nations. Their imaginations raced, buoyed by optimism. After the horrors of the flood, it seemed impossible that any would turn against the Almighty again.

But Noah watched in trepidation, knowing the beast that lies within the human heart. He witnessed its ferocity in the days before the flood, and he knew that no perversion was too distant from a heart turned away from its Maker. But he shook off the misgivings. Today was a day for gratefulness, a day for celebration.

The rainbow receded, and isolated caps of dry land began to appear. For now, they would settle high, almost within the shadow of the ark. Every day Noah worked, building a vineyard and a place for his wife and sons, but his children soon bore children of their own. "Soon we'll go down," he would say.

His family spread out in the foothills. The hills below the mountains of Ararat were plenteous, but his sons' sons seemed to grow exponentially in number. Only a few decades later, Noah could not remember all his grandchildren's names; the hills were becoming overpopulated. The time had finally come. Noah called for a great feast.

As the people gathered, Noah told of the insidious evil that had saturated the earth. He told of God's command to build an ark. He told of the great flood. He told of corruption, how it had seized every human heart with vile intentions. He wept, recovered himself, and then paused. Resolve passed across his face.

"The Lord commanded that we go forth into the earth to fill it. The time has come: you must leave this place and settle the earth. I have grown far too old for such a journey. My three sons will lead you. Follow them, for I have instructed them to obey God's command."

Finally, the journey had begun. As they traveled, uncertainty plagued the family clans. Soon their familiar hills fell behind, becoming blue and hazy in the distance. Where would they go? Would they be scattered into oblivion? Would the stronger clans rise up to dominate the weaker? The future was as uncertain as each day's supply of food and water.

Just when the people had begun to think the journey would never end, a broad plain opened before them. Situated between the Tigris and Euphrates rivers, the land was like an apparition. There was water, game, and plenty of everything they might ever need. It was a long debate, but Shem, Ham, and Japheth decided this fruitful plain in the land of Shinar would provide a good—though, they stressed, temporary—place to settle.

The Land of Shinar

Shinar's plain was more fertile than anyone could have imagined. The clans worked together to establish agriculture and a steady food supply. Roads were built, tools and occupations invented. New opportunities emerged that were previously unheard of. The people began to dream of what the future might hold if they remained together. It seemed nothing was out of reach while they united in purpose. The economy grew; fortunes were amassed.

A new generation arose with very different values from those of their forefathers. Endless barrels of wine subtly dulled their senses. They feasted indulgently on the abundance of the land's provision. Forgotten was the Creator's command to fill the earth; ignored were the sons of Noah who had taken up their father's old mantra: "Soon. Soon we will go." Even more children were being born and raised far from the shadow of the bulky, rotting ark. Whispers spread that Noah himself was just an old fable.

After many years in Shinar, Shem and Japheth, believing God's command had been too long neglected, summoned the leadership of the city to continue the migration. But it was too late. The council was convinced that their burgeoning civilization had grown far too advanced to follow a silly fable. It was decided that the days of migration were over. The people had fallen in love with the glory of Shinar.

A message was sent. When Noah learned that his descendants had settled and refused to continue the migration, he responded immediately. Urging the people to disperse, to settle other parts of the earth, he spoke of the great blessing they would experience in obeying the Lord, but also of the devastating consequences of disobedience.

Noah's words were met with resistance and stirred even greater defiance. Again and again he sent messengers, but his urgings prompted only bitter mocking. The younger generations ridiculed the senile fossil in the mountains who seemed to think he ruled over them. They were their own rulers now and would certainly not tolerate old-fashioned ways and fear-inducing superstition.

The people of Shinar saw no reason to listen to Noah or his sons. Their progressive society had ascended above the traditional views of God. Freedom and moral license had become the dominant persuasion of the day. Irrational devotion to the God of Noah was a threat to the new civilization's social trends. Such a religion would certainly curtail the free-flowing economy; such impositions would impede original thought and creativity. Rather than yield to the pleas of Noah, they determined to pursue the seductive enticement of a new breed of leaders. And so the human race fell under the spell of the woman Semiramis.

SEMIRAMIS

Semiramis had captured the people's imagination.[1] She was perfect, the most seductive and radiant woman in all Shinar. Her shape was irresistible; her movements shattered the strongest men. No woman of legend has ever surpassed her. The women of Shinar all desired to be her, and the men to be with her.

Not a first daughter, not even the daughter of a councilman, Semiramis's beauty and intelligence had made avenues for her into realms far beyond the dreams of her peers. The great religious leaders were often found drinking wine in her company. But only the most powerful men found their way to her bed. Semiramis' alluring powers of seduction were matched only by her insatiable drive for power.

She convinced the people that it was simplistic to think that there could only be one God. To be truly free meant total freedom in worship. She told them that gods inhabited every aspect of creation. With her teachings, she blurred the lines that distinguished spiritual realties. Semiramis had awakened the dawn of false religion.

At one time, sexual promiscuity had been rare, but the more the people defied the Creator in their pursuit of "progressive" views of spirituality, the more outrageous their sexual exploits became. They lusted after every manner of pleasure. Soon, one after another began to abandon

---

[1]   Semiramis was a legendary Assyrian queen.

the moral restraints of their forefathers to pursue the carnal passions of a new generation. New thoughts about the creation, new definitions of God, and new experimentation in unbridled licentiousness began to proliferate throughout the land.

The Faithful

Within a few short years, traditional social mores had been demolished. What previously seemed unthinkable was playing out on every street corner and in every house. In disgust, Noah's sons, Shem and Japheth, met secretly one evening.

"We should take all who will still listen and continue the migration," Japheth said."

Shem sat stunned. It would be giving up, leaving all their wayward children's children to fend for themselves, to grope their way through the godless fog of idolatry without a single compass of truth. Tears streaked his face. "I do not want to let them go, Japheth. I cannot give up on them."

"If we stay, we may lose even more. Semiramis' seduction is far more powerful than we realize, Shem."

"I simply cannot consent to this without word from Father. I will send a messenger."

Noah's answer was unmistakable. *Do not forsake your people. Who will remain to intercede? Remember Abel, remember Enoch, remember your great-grandfather Methuselah. You are being offered in mercy, by the hand of God, to your wayward children. He will act to save when you call on His name.*

The lives of the faithful became very difficult. Not only must they walk in holy ways through lawless streets, they must warn of judgment and proclaim God to a people who already mocked their tent-living and moderate pleasures. The faithful were scorned as outsiders, as strangers.

There was no middle ground. Those who did not draw closer to God became further intoxicated with the lifestyle of Shinar. And Semiramis, whom Japheth had expected to persecute them, lured and tempted them instead. All the wealth, all the luxury Shinar afforded could be theirs and their children's, if they would simply yield. The humblest of the faithful withstood and preached repentance; those who thought themselves strong fell before her corruption. Prayer became the dividing line between the two. Only extreme vigilance in prayer kept the heart from falling into decadent trappings. Intercession on behalf of wayward people was also a means of grace that preserved the faithful through the fires of Shinar.

Semiramis despised those who withstood her, who lived in a state of readiness to migrate, who preached to the people of their disobedience and the consequences of rebellion against the God of Noah. But she did not fear them, for she knew the people were already far too enchanted with mystical spiritualism and self-indulgence to be anything but suspicious of Noah's message.

Something strange was stirring in the land of Shinar. No one could articulate the impulse that began to stir beneath the surface of their culture, driving them onward and uniting them in vision and purpose. An unseen force was at work, merging and moving them as ocean undercurrents drive the ships on the surface. Behind the veil of what could be seen lurked a malevolent power paving the way for Shinar's new king.

NIMROD

Nimrod was the grandson of Ham, son of the leader of the tribal council, Cush. Prowess and cunning were his inheritance; his skill with sword, spear, and bow were unmatched. His thirst for glory was insatiable. Nimrod, renowned as a mighty hunter, had trained his murderous eye on political power and stalked it relentlessly.

But Shinar had already bowed to another. Semiramis held the public's affection in her seductive grip. She ruled the land by proxy through the "mighty" council. She alone held the keys to the power he coveted.

Nimrod had come into his own, and Semiramis had taken note of his swift rise to power. The gods were with him. The incredible potential of harnessing his violent bloodlust for her own political expansion and security intoxicated her. Their union in marriage would create an indomitable alliance. And so, with a great feast of celebration, the approval of the people, and the envy of the council, Nimrod took Semiramis as his wife. While the people danced and drank deep into the night, Nimrod knew he had successfully consolidated his power.

The King of Babylon

His place at Semiramis' side secured, Nimrod began voicing his own agenda, one very different from hers. Hoping that he could convince his new wife of the golden era that could be achieved, Nimrod instead found that Semiramis dismissed his ideas. She had married him to reinforce the power and influence of her throne. She had heralded sexual experimentation and spiritual relativism under the banner of tolerance for all, and her progressive ideas had given her power beyond anything imaginable. But her husband now began questioning her ideas in private: "How can we progress as a unified people when everyone is so soft and spineless? They must be led, controlled, to reach their full potential. They desire it, you know. Human achievement, glory, and power."

Soon Nimrod's private ideas were cloaked in deception and transformed into public propaganda. Great promises tapped into the population's latent fears—of death, of insignificance, of being forgotten—and he began to win away from Semiramis the very hearts she had opened for him. A devoted following soon developed, spurred on by his vocal group of henchmen. His loyal hunting companions had become a powerful band of political brutes. Those who resisted him found themselves intimidated into quiet submission, and with the support of his small army of thugs he quickly rose in power and influence, until Semiramis was almost forgotten.

Nimrod convinced the people that Semiramis was trying to keep them from the true glory of their human potential. His speech was inflammatory, his presence electrifying. He accused the Creator God of maliciously destroying their forefathers and secretly conspiring to do it again. He convinced them that it was by their own courage they had come so far, and only he could lead them on to even greater heights of peace and unity. Spiritual confusion had so deluded the people that they soon believed every word Nimrod spoke. Within a few months they made him king.

The Tower

Soon the newly appointed king saw need of changes in the government. The long-standing tribal council, corrupt though it had been, was dissolved. The old freedoms and license the people had enjoyed under Semiramis became counterproductive to his aims. Nimrod's small band of political henchmen was expanded into an army. All the settlements of Shinar would now answer to Nimrod directly. This king would make every decision exclusively, and those who resisted him would suffer. Tyranny was the only option if Nimrod wanted to lead the people completely out of any remaining fear of God and into total dependence on his power. The people, deluded and hungry for glory, followed him willingly. Nimrod's name had a spectacular meaning: "let us revolt." Shinar had become the epicenter of the earth's defiance.

Now the gods began speaking to Nimrod in dreams. Night after night he dreamt of a great tower rising from the midst of a golden city and reaching into the clouds. It was a beautiful heavenly sanctuary, built for the gods' residence. One pivotal night, the greatest of these gods appeared to him and commanded him to build a city and tower on earth, just like the one he had seen in heaven. This sky-scraping temple-tower would be a gateway for the gods to confer unimaginable power and glory on the king of men.

In a thunderous, eloquent speech Nimrod announced his plan. They would build a city and tower to attest to their own greatness.

> Come, let us build for ourselves a city and a tower with its top in the heavens, and let us make a name for ourselves, lest we be dispersed over the face of the whole earth.
>
> —Genesis 11:4

The people from all of Shinar's settlements came together, determined to succeed in the greatest endeavor in all of history. Brick by brick the tower took shape, a new city rising around it. Never before had so many labored in such united purpose. Never before had the stakes been this high. Not only would human history remember their renown, their efforts would bring them into the very realm of the gods and immortality. The tower was named Babel, "gateway of the gods," for it would reach into the heavens and provide a portal whereby the gods could descend upon the earth. The spiritual realm would be joined to the earthly realm. The Tower of Babel was nothing less than an invitation for demons to seize control of the earth.

Nimrod's empire centered on the new, pristine city of Babel. Political, religious, and commercial power sprang from the seat of imperial authority, and no citizen of Shinar considered going elsewhere to conduct business. River ports and markets for trading created a bustling economic powerhouse; within decades, no other city in the plain could match its accelerated growth. Every surrounding settlement that hoped to share in Shinar's prosperity was infected with the culture and spirit of Babel. And year by year the tower grew taller.

Finally, in a climactic act of human arrogance, Nimrod exalted himself as god. Those who refused to worship him were considered enemies of the state, barred from the city of Babel. All who were deceived (as most were, deluded and conditioned by decades of tyranny and lies) made images of him to worship in their homes. Soon, when the tower was completed, he would be enthroned upon its peak.

God's faithful servants had taken no part in the building of Babel, giving themselves instead to prayer. Unable to meet openly, they came together in small groups spread out across the region. Tiny pockets of light flickered in Babel's darkness, voices supplicating their Creator, pleading for His visitation. A unified voice cried out for the Lord to come. They knew that if He did not intervene now, the city of Babel would introduce sin and demonic activity into the world at such a level as to provoke the full strength of God's wrath.

Though no one could see it, the prayers of the saints were prevailing. God had heard every cry. His judgment would be swift but merciful. Without judgment, the world would quickly degenerate into the wickedness that had prevailed before the great flood. The Lord could see beyond Babel. He knew that the power at work behind this nefarious city would be fully manifested at the end of time.

The Visitation

What began as just another day in Babel suddenly changed without warning. Clouds gathered and deepened, rumblings played antiphonally from east to west, the shadows were darkest black, and where sunlight broke through, it was too brilliant to be endured.

The Lord appeared in the clouds, coming near to look down on the city and the tower the people had made. With a mighty voice He spoke to the heavenly hosts accompanying Him.

> Behold, they are one people, and they have all one language, and this is only the beginning of what they will do. And nothing that they propose to do will now be impossible for them.
> —Genesis 11:6

God had devised a plan to disperse the people into

all the earth without having to devastate them. His hand would not take one life. In a single instant, the years-long cry of the faithful was answered; in one day the dispersion had begun. God touched the mouths of the people and changed the language they spoke. Family by family, a different tongue came out when the people tried to speak. Neighbor turned in fear from neighbor, manager from laborer. Work halted abruptly, sacrifices ceased. Nimrod raged in his palace, but none could understand his words.

The city and tower had been paralyzed. Each of Shem, Ham, and Japheth's grandsons spoke different languages, and their families with them. Finding it impossible to continue collaborating in a single economy, government, or religion, they left the city group by group according to common language. And so the Lord scattered the people over the face of the earth, to do as He had originally commanded.

The demonic power at work in Shinar had been defeated but there would come a new day and time when another city would rise to unite the whole earth. Nimrod's vision of the city and tower was not the end, but just the beginning of Babylon.

PART I

THEOLOGICAL FOUNDATIONS

O N E
BABYLON

By the waters of Babylon, there we sat down
and wept, when we remembered Zion.
—Psalm 137:1

WHERE NOAH AND THE TOWER OF BABEL end, a far
longer journey begins. On the heels of the eleventh chapter of Genesis, the Bible introduces a native of Babylonia who would change the course of history. This person
wasn't your average Babylonian. The same region that
produced the Tower of Babel gave birth to the man whose
seed would one day come to bless all the nations: Abraham. It is surprising that one of the most significant figures
of the Old Testament was originally from the land of the
Chaldeans.[1] To put it in modern terms, Abraham was born
an Iraqi.

Something distinguished Abraham from those around
him. When the call of God came, he didn't hesitate. His
friends and family were perfectly content with life in Babylonia. No one could understand why he would want to

---

[1] See Genesis 11:31. We will revisit the Chaldeans in Part III as King
Nebuchadnezzar takes the stage.

leave. But Abraham desired something more. Something in his spiritual DNA made him a stranger in his native land.

What was it about Abraham that made him willing to leave the familiar comforts of his home and follow God into the great unknown? The answer is simple—citizenship. Abraham was a resident of the celestial city. His citizenship in the city of God made him a stranger on earth.

> They were strangers and exiles on the earth.
> —Hebrews 11:13

Abraham journeyed through life in search of something greater. He possessed something that made him different from those around him—an inexpressible yearning for another place. When Abraham packed up and left his country, everyone thought he was crazy. But what they couldn't see was the living vision God had placed deep within his heart. Once touched by this vision, Abraham was never the same.

None of the comforts and pleasures of Babylonia could ever satiate Abraham. Everything he had experienced in Shinar had left him strangely empty. Only one thing could satisfy Abraham's longing. His heart was defined by an unrelenting desire for another city.

> He was looking forward to the city that has foundations, whose designer and builder is God.
> —Hebrews 11:10

The Thread

Abraham wasn't the only stranger. In fact, he was just one in a long line. The Bible tells of an ancient tradition of sojourners who found themselves strangely out of place in the earth. These individuals refused to barter divine destiny for the comforts and pleasures of the world—like Zerubbabel, whose name literally meant "stranger in Babylon," or, more notably, like John the Baptist, who emerged from the Judean wilderness preaching an uncompromising message of repentance to a nation that had lost its identity under the influence of Rome.

A holy ancestral thread is woven through the generation of exiles who returned from Babylonian captivity in order to rebuild the temple in Jerusalem. It continues through the first generation of Christians who overcame the corruption and oppression of Rome. This family line of strangers in Babylon will continue through the final generation of Christians who will overcome Babylon the Great in the end times.

> Therefore God is not ashamed to be called their
> God, for he has prepared for them a city.
> —Hebrews 11:16b

As the Church, we enjoy a rich spiritual heritage. We come from a long line of sojourners. Saints through the ages have obediently served God, living as aliens in the earth. We belong to an ancient tradition revealed in the pages of the Bible, a tradition that has critical implications for us today. But we dare not merely hear the story; we must tell the story, and, most importantly, live the story.

The first part of the story has now been told. The original metropolis that came to embody corporate rebellion against God culminated in an unfinished tower. God swept down and thwarted Nimrod's plan to unite the human race against God. We will revisit the Tower of Babel in greater detail, but before we do, we must establish a certain fundamental theological framework if we are to understand why the Tower of Babel happened in the first place. To understand what is happening *in* the story, we must first understand what is happening *behind* the story.

Understanding Babylon

Babylon is an often used but frequently misunderstood expression. From its place in popular music to its prevalence among conspiracy theorists, few terms have been employed so ambiguously. But the biblical idea of Babylon goes much farther than a rhetorical tag for the materialism of our day or a buzzword for anti-government groups. What the Bible teaches about the scope and power of Babylon will awaken the Christian heart to the sober reality of the hour in which we live and the days that lie ahead.

History tells of world empires based solely upon single cities. Unlike the ancient empires of Egypt, Assyria, and Persia that were named after the nations from which they sprang, certain empires have been based entirely on a single city that served as the global nerve-center for every facet of human civilization.[2] Both the Babylonian Empire and the Roman Empire were named after a city rather than a nation. No one has ever heard of the Chaldean Empire or the Latin Empire for a reason.[3] Both first-century Rome and ancient Babylon were single cities that became so

---

[2] Each of the aforementioned empires all had several different influential cities that served different functions as economic, religious, and military centers. It can be argued that seven kingdoms of Revelation 17:10 are Egypt, Assyria, Babylon, Persia, Greece, Rome, and Babylon the Great (see Thomas, *Revelation 8–22*, 297). This would mean that each of these kingdoms were manifestations of Babylon. However, this is a much debated and somewhat controversial prophetic interpretation. I will only deal with the cities that the Bible explicitly cites as being a Babylon.

[3] Latium was an ancient region of the Italian peninsula.

powerful and influential that they dominated the world.[4] To understand it in modern terms, imagine a single city possessing the economic power of New York, the political power of Washington DC, the cultural influence of Hollywood, and the religious influence of Jerusalem.

The Mystery

From Genesis to Revelation, Babylon is threaded throughout Scripture. The Bible refers to Babylon in eighteen different books. The longest Old Testament passage of prophecy is the foretelling of Babylon's fall in Jeremiah 50–51. The longest passage of prophecy in the New Testament is John's vision of the great harlot in Revelation 17–18.

But even with the vast amount of information the Bible contains regarding Babylon, we must recognize that this subject is fraught with difficulty for a number of reasons. During the apocalyptic vision in the book of Revelation, the apostle John saw that great mystery was woven into this reality. We must recognize that there is still undisclosed information about Babylon the Great. In other words, we do not have all the information we need for a perfect picture of eschatological Babylon.[5]

Adding to the controversy surrounding the topic of Babylon are questions of geography. While debate will continue regarding the location of eschatological Babylon, we must bear in mind that history has demonstrated

---

[4] Not every powerful city has the distinction of being a Babylon. Only when it becomes the center of global prominence and the maelstrom of human decadence and defiance against God does the Bible label it a Babylon. None of the cities of ancient Assyria or the great cities of ancient Egypt are ever explicitly referred to in the Bible as being a Babylon.

[5] Eschatology means the study of the end times.

that Babylon transcends geography.[6] Just as the antichrist spirit can function through different individuals over the course of history, yet will culminate in one final man of sin,[7] the spirit of Babylon is a power that has worked within different civilizations, but will ultimately be fully expressed through one city in the final years of the present age.

Understanding what is behind the power of Babylon is made even more difficult by the number of natural and supernatural variables in the equation. Babylon will emerge as a city that serves as the hub of a worldwide religious, economic, and political network. Yet the human factor is only the surface reality; below the natural veneer, supernatural demonic powers drive human society toward satanic objectives. The commingling of natural and supernatural elements makes deciphering this mystery extremely challenging.

The future Babylon is shrouded in great mystery, but we can gain tremendous insight into it by looking backward through time. George Ladd writes, "The great harlot sits upon a succession of empires. She found her embodiment in historical Babylon, in the first century in historical Rome, and at the end of the age in eschatological Babylon."[8] If we cannot get a perfect picture of the future Babylon the Great, we can look to the Bible and human history to show us the Babylons of the past; we must trace its history and follow its development.

---

[6] First-century Rome illustrates that a "Babylon" can be manifested in a different area of the world from its original site.

[7] 1 John 2:18 tells us of the "many antichrists" already in the world and widens the scope of an antichrist to include heretics. 2 Thessalonians 2:3–5 prophesies of the ultimate Antichrist who is to be revealed. Specific examples of antichrists include Nimrod, Nebuchadnezzar, Antiochus Epiphanes, Nero, and Adolf Hitler.

[8] Ladd, *Revelation of John*, 228. Also see Revelation 18:2.

The Template

In Revelation 17–18, the Bible gives us the fullest picture of Babylon the Great. Nearly 2,000 years ago, the apostle John saw the great city dominating the earth in the end times. He was given a behind-the-scenes look at the demonic power at work behind Babylon. From this prophetic depiction, there are at least eight characteristics that mark Babylon in its full manifestation:[9]

1. She is the originator and progenitor of false religion.[10]

2. She is enthroned upon the nations (Rev. 17:15).

3. She is the center of global commerce (Rev. 18:3b).

4. She is the ultimate symbol of human rebellion against God (Rev. 18:7).

5. She intoxicates the nations with sexual immorality (Rev. 17:2b).[11]

---

[9] This is not meant to be a comprehensive list. There are certainly more than eight characteristics, but this is my best attempt at simplifying a very complicated phenomenon in a way that accurately reflects similarities through time.

[10] By being called the "mother of prostitutes and of earth's abominations" (Rev. 17:5), Babylon is identified as the progenitor of idolatry and false religion. The prostitution in view here is not primarily fornication but the spiritual harlotry so often denounced in the Old Testament. However, gross immorality is a primary outgrowth of spiritual harlotry.

[11] The literal application of "sexual immorality" is woven into the same fabric as the metaphorical spiritual idolatry of the previous verses. Immorality and idolatry are fundamentally interconnected. The Bible uses the terms almost interchangeably. "The prostitute is lavishly adorned with gold and precious stones. In her hand she holds a golden cup that promises a heady draught of carnal satisfaction. Its contents, however, are quite otherwise. The cup is full of the 'abominable things and the filth of her adulteries.' Moral corruption and all manner of ceremonial uncleanness are what she offers." Mounce, *The NICNT: The Book of Revelation*, 310.

6. She becomes obsessed with persecuting God's saints (Rev. 17:6).

7. She is empowered by and paves the way for the Antichrist.[12]

8. Her destruction comes quickly and completely (Rev. 18:10).

These characteristics have been evident every time Babylon has arisen through history. Beginning with ancient Babel, the birthplace of Babylon, this demonically inspired phenomenon has been expressed again and again with striking similarities. The Babylonian Empire, the Roman Empire, and the coming Antichrist empire all bear these marks.

Every human civilization is unique, yet these recurring characteristics prove that something else is at work behind Babylon—something inhuman. What is it that makes the manifestation of the very different Babylons so consistent in character throughout the ages? Thousands of years and total ethnic distinction separate Babel, Babylon, Rome, and Babylon the Great, yet there is a striking resemblance between each city's power, influence, and fate. To understand the factors behind this odd consistency throughout history, we must look back at the progression of Satan's will to power[13] and God's plan to restore all things.

---

[12] Revelation 17:3 describes one of the most striking characteristics of Babylon as one who rides on the back of the Antichrist. But this relationship is reversed in Revelation 17:16 when the Antichrist destroys the great city. See Part 5.

[13] "The will to become like God is the will to power, to shape lives and determine destinies. The basic urge which drives human beings to gain power over others is a perversion of the creature's basic instinct to acknowledge God and to acknowledge dependence on God." Dunn, *Theology of Paul the Apostle*, 114–115.

T W O

SATAN'S PLAN TO DOMINATE THE EARTH

LUST FOR POWER IS AS OLD as the earth itself. In fact, it is older. The quest to bring the entire human race into subjection has taken many forms through history. But to understand what is behind this unrelenting struggle for power, we must look beyond human history. We must look to the Scriptures to gain insight into the original heart of darkness from which tyranny flows, and see that what began in the garden of Eden will culminate with the Antichrist.

Beginning in the Garden

> You said in your heart, "I will ascend to heaven
> … I will ascend above the heights of the clouds;
> I will make myself like the Most High."
> —Isaiah 14:13a, 14

When Satan arose in war against God, he and his hordes were overcome and expelled from God's presence. But Satan's cosmic rebellion found a new expression. If he could not rule the realm of the Uncreated One, he would do the next best thing—he would rule the realm of the created. Since Satan would never have the celestial city, he would concentrate his malice on creating a terrestrial one.[1] Satan's war continued on in the temptation of Adam.

The very same blasphemous desire that had resulted in Satan's expulsion from heaven would be the enticement that would work to exile Adam and Eve from the garden of Eden. Satan's desire to be "like the Most High" intoxicated Adam and Eve with delusions of grandeur. Like Satan, the human race embraced rebellion as the avenue to "become as God." Adam and Eve swallowed Satan's bait and ate the fruit from the only tree in the garden that God commanded them not to eat from: the Tree of Knowledge.

Satan beguiled them without a single threat. The soothing promise of greater power and glory was enough. The temptation to revolt against God—in favor of human progress—was first introduced in the garden. Once Satan had convinced Adam and Eve that human glory was to be preferred above the glory of God, he had already prevailed. It was here that the foundation stones of Babylon were being laid in the human heart—stones that would one day build a city.

The same underlying motive that drove Adam and Eve to eat the forbidden fruit provided the inspiration for the Tower of Babel. The satanic desire to become God is the thread that runs from Eden to Babylon. The spirit of rebellion recorded in Genesis 11 is described in Psalm 2:

> Why do the nations rage and the peoples plot in vain? The kings of the earth set themselves, and the rulers take counsel together, against the Lord and against his anointed.
>
> —Psalm 2:1–2

---

[1]   That Babylon is the false New Jerusalem will become evident in Part 5.

The human confederacy with Satan's campaign to "ascend to heaven and become as the most high" can take many forms. It can look like eating fruit, as was the case with Adam and Eve. Or it can look like building sky-scraping architecture. To the human eye it can look beautiful, alluring, and inspiring. And for those who don't know the difference, it can even look like the true religion. But whatever guise the outward expression assumes, the crusade to take God's place is the cornerstone of Babylon.

The Kingdom of Darkness

Besides his title as the king of Babylon,[2] Satan is also known as "the ruler of this world" (Jn. 12:31, 14:30, 16:11). But how did Satan gain this position when God never gave him authority to rule the earth? The privilege to have dominion over the earth had been given exclusively to Adam. This divine mandate was to be fulfilled in relationship with and in submission to God (Gen. 1:26). The devil had to access Adam's position in order to govern. Satan could only become the "god of this age" (2 Cor. 4:4) by usurping Adam's God-given human authority.

To gain power, Satan extends his rule through partnership with fallen humans. Only by means of human agents can Satan's kingdom expand. Humans are the foot soldiers who give hands and feet to demonic agendas. Without the cooperation of human hearts, Satan is without recourse. The curses spoken by humans, the cruelty of

---

[2] Isaiah 14:3–22 is a taunt against the king of Babylon. In this prophetic oracle, Isaiah declares that the remnant of Israel will take up "this proverb against the king of Babylon" (14:3). But the teachings of the Church have firmly established verses 13 and 14 as referring to Satan's rebellion and consequent expulsion from heaven. Thus, the interconnection between Satan and the king of Babylon is scripturally explicit. See. Boyd, *God at War*, 157–160.

human behavior, the evil of human hearts—all of these are the vehicles by which the kingdom of darkness enters the human realm. Sin is the confederacy of men and devils; it is the gateway for Satan's influence in every domain of social, political, economic, and religious activity. The more sin abounds, the more the spiritual atmosphere becomes rife with demonic activity, and the more the kingdom of hell takes root in the earth. In other words, tempting humans to sin is the gateway to Satan's government of the world.

Demonic principalities introduce Satan's agenda to promote sin into human society at a systemic level. There is no question of the incessant influence of demons at the individual level. The temptation, discouragement, and lies we all face are just a few examples of how Satan's minions are at work in our daily lives.[3] But the Bible teaches that evil principalities direct world empires.[4] When the apostle Paul refers to the cosmic rulers and authorities of the "darkness of this age" (Eph. 6:12), he is describing the satanic power that is able to influence entire societies.[5]

The Antichrist

Satan's primary objective is not only to rule the earth, but also to be worshiped like God. All who surround God are awed into lovesick worship. Every eye that sees His transcendent beauty must bow and cry "Holy! Holy! Holy!" Heaven consists of wholehearted worshipers of God. In fact, you can't inhabit heaven without being one!

The archangel Lucifer found this out the hard way. When pride overcame his heart and his desire to become

[3] For a classic literary example of demonic influence on the individual level, see C. S. Lewis' *The Screwtape Letters*.
[4] Dan. 10:13, 20.
[5] Boyd, *God at War*, 270–276.

like the Most High overpowered him, Satan couldn't tolerate all of heaven worshiping God. But his revolt failed and he turned his demonic gaze toward the earth. His wicked heart became bent on being worshiped by the nations.

The devil's final objective is to enslave every human being on earth to worship him. It isn't enough that humans are worshiping lesser demons; through the Antichrist, Satan will one day demand that all the inhabitants of earth bow to him alone.[6] This is the ultimate objective of Satan's agenda. The apostle Paul tells the Thessalonian church that the Antichrist will oppose and exalt "himself against every so-called god or object of worship" (2 Thes. 2:4). Make no mistake; the devil's endgame is to displace tolerance, religious syncretism, and idolatry with an entirely intolerant and exclusive religion in the form of emperor worship. This will be the Antichrist's ultimate objective; he will not tolerate the worship of anything else.

History attests to countless individuals who have given their hearts to the antichrist spirit, in a foreshadowing of the Antichrist. The insane Seleucid king, Antiochus IV, who desecrated the Jewish temple and viciously persecuted the Jewish people in 167 BC, tops the list. In many ways, the prideful Chaldean king, Nebuchadnezzar, prefigured the Antichrist.[7] The Roman emperor, Nero, whose riotous lust for blood resulted in the persecution of Christians in AD 64–67, is another. Many other men in some way or another fit the profile of the Antichrist, but none of them have fulfilled the prophecy entirely.[8] These are only a few examples

[6] Rev. 13:15.

[7] "Nebuchadnezzar, king of kings, who demanded universal worship, who set up an image of himself, and decreed that all should worship it under pain of death, etc., manifestly pointed forward to the Man of Sin..." Pink, *The Antichrist*, 230.

[8] For a list of biblical types of the Antichrist, see Pink, *The Antichrist,* 215f.

of how the antichrist spirit can influence powerful political leaders to commit horrendous offenses against God and His people.

Free societies do not welcome tyranny, but given the right influence, they will succumb to it. As a society departs from the values that made it free, it grows ever closer to enslaving itself to a tyrant. Consider first-century Rome when the empire was swept with optimism that the Emperor Nero would usher in a new golden age.[9] The romantic feelings lasted until Nero's autocratic agenda dissolved the powers of the Roman Senate and his lusts led to the burning of Rome. Or consider twentieth-century Germany, where a "modern," civilized nation embraced Judeophobia.[10] This irrational notion that Jews were responsible for all social and economic ills made the most murderous atrocity in history possible—the Final Solution was allowed by a country deceived and bound by the power of a satanically inspired tyrant. The free societies of first-century Rome and twentieth-century Germany had to believe the demonic, political visions of Nero and Hitler before giving their allegiance. In other words, the human heart must be conditioned over time before welcoming an antichrist leader. The frightening thing is that this conditioning can be imperceptible.[11]

[9]   Champlin, *Nero*, 74.

[10] There is little doubt that without the preexisting anti-Semitism that pervaded early twentieth-century Europe, the Holocaust would have been impossible. "The Nazis did not need to invent the image of 'the Jew' as a usurer, blasphemer, traitor, ritual murderer, dangerous conspirator against Christendom, or a deadly threat to the foundations of morality." Wistrich, *Hitler and the Holocaust*, xiv.

[11] "Little by little this spirit of license, finding a home, imperceptibly penetrates into manners and customs; whence, issuing with greater force, it invades contracts between man and man, and from contracts goes on to laws and constitutions, in utter recklessness, end-

The Enslavement of Sin

What brings rebellious humans under the power of a vicious tyrant? It's difficult to imagine an anti-establishment flower child of the 1960s bowing in worship to a world leader like Adolf Hitler. But that, in essence, is what the Bible teaches will happen in the end times: licentiousness will give way to a form of totalitarianism that not even George Orwell could have imagined.

American culture has made it easy to underestimate the sinful power of human rebellion. On the surface, rebellion appears to be nothing more than a way to express individualism. But there is more to being a rebel than its depiction by James Dean. The 1960s were a time in America when rebelling against authority seeped into mainstream culture. We have all seen films from that era of protesters and concertgoers dressed in tie-dyed clothing, believing they were experiencing true freedom by casting off every restraint. But embracing rebellion against God is serious business; at its core, it is high treason. The inner reality behind human rebellion is an allegiance with the primeval rebel. Satan was the first to rebel, and those who choose to resist God join his cause.

The inner reality behind rebellion explains the ultimate outworking of tyranny. It may seem difficult to imagine why lawless humans would willingly bow to a tyrant, but the answer is simple. The outward manifestation of emperor worship is merely the result of an inner transaction that has already taken effect. Lawless humans will worship antichrist leaders because they have already willingly joined themselves with Satan at the heart level. The seemingly innocuous embracement of rebellion leads a human heart

ing at last, Socrates, by an overthrow of all rights, private as well as public." Plato, *The Portable Plato*, 420.

directly under the enslaving power of evil. On the outside, a human who has embraced rebellion may appear to be entirely out of anyone's control, but inwardly he or she is bound with dark chains.

THREE

THE RESTORATION OF ALL THINGS

> I will build my church, and the gates of hell shall
> not prevail against it.
>
> —Matthew 16:18

ALTHOUGH SATAN RULES FALLEN MEN, he is merely a pawn in the scope of God's eternal purpose. We must never forget that God is in total control of everything. Above all the conspiracies of devils and men, our God reigns supreme. He knows every event before it occurs and works everything together in His plan to glorify His name. Even the defiant city of Babylon itself was a God-ordained servant.[1]

In spite of all his raging defiance, the devil will always play right into the Lord's hands. God is not pacing about in heaven fretting over the threat that Satan poses. Certainly Satan is an enemy of God's work in the earth. But let's not forget God is still God. The Lord knew every move Satan would make before He created him. When this age closes, God will dispose of Satan without delay or toil.[2]

This doesn't mean that Satan isn't powerful; he has been

[1] Hab. 1:12.
[2] Rev. 20:1–2, 10.

given tremendous power in this age. He rages around the created order, stealing, killing, and destroying (Jn. 10:10). Hatred for all is the foul air he breathes. By deception he wages war to the death and wields temptation like a champion's sword. The power of sin and death are his greatest allies. Multitudes of heaven's angels, now fallen, are at his command.[3] No one in the lineage of the first Adam is a match for him. Satan can inspire nations to war and individuals to unimaginable sin.[4] He can direct the highest affairs of human politics and economics. Though he is a pawn to God, Satan is a nightmare for fallen humans.

And while Satan has busied himself with malicious objectives that will never ultimately succeed, God has been executing an ultimate plan that can never be thwarted. Before the foundations of the earth were laid, God ordained heaven and earth to be one. In the beginning, the garden of Eden was the place where Creator and created related without hindrance. Everything changed with the entrance of sin. The unity of heaven and earth was shattered and the kingdom of darkness took hold. But the fundamental breach incurred by the fall was not between the spiritual realm of heaven and the natural realm of earth; the fundamental breach was between a holy God and a now-sinful human race.

God was not taken aback by this tragic turn. While Satan has sought to release the power of hell on earth through human sin, God has been executing a sovereign plan to redeem creation by bringing the kingdom of heaven back to earth. The apostle Paul writes of God's sovereign plan to unite heaven and earth in his letter to the church

---

[3] Rev. 12:9.
[4] For example: Armageddon and Judas Iscariot, respectively.

at Ephesus:[5]

> Making known to us the mystery of his will, according to his purpose, which he set forth in Christ as a plan for the fullness of time, to unite all things in him, things in heaven and things on earth.
>
> —Ephesians 1:9–10

The apostle Paul declares that God has revealed a sovereign plan to reunite heaven and earth in the fullness of time. God declares Himself the sole proprietor of the only remedy to the fall. He willed and purposed this plan entirely within Himself. But how could God repair the irreparable? How could the Holy One ever again welcome sinful humans into His presence and embrace a world that had joined Satan's rebellion? The inconceivable answer to this incomprehensible question was that God would bring heaven and earth together in His Messiah.

The Remedy for the Fall

God's sovereign plan to restore the kingdom of God to earth was revealed to Jacob in a stunning dream. While on a long journey, the ancient patriarch stopped in order to get some sleep.

> And he dreamed, and behold there was a ladder set up on the earth, and the top of it reached to heaven. And behold, the angels of God were ascending and descending on it! And behold, the LORD stood above it.
>
> —Genesis 28:12–13

[5] The Christian view of uniting heaven and earth has nothing to do with utopianism. Human effort to achieve utopia in this age is an underlying ideology of Babylon, not the Bible.

Jacob was invited to take a look deep within God's heart. The Lord was grieved over the chasm that sin had created between heaven and earth. In the garden of Eden, God had interacted with His creation face to face. But since the fall, there had been an insurmountable separation between a holy God and sinful man. Mankind's greatest need was to bridge that separation. And the answer to that need could never be a human attempt to reach into heaven. No amount of sinful human effort could ever reach God. Unless the Creator had a sovereign plan to reach down from heaven to men, all hope would be lost. What mankind needed most was not another prideful attempt to reach up as they had at Babel, but a humble-hearted God who would lovingly reach down. Enter Jacob's ladder. Jacob saw God's provision for man's need. He saw the true gateway of God—the Lord's remedy for the fall—and named the place of his vision accordingly. It wasn't Babel; it was Bethel, "the house of God."

Bethel was the sole answer to mankind's greatest need. What the human race needed more than anything else was for God to once again dwell in the earth. Since the fall, sin had created a chasm between Creator and created. After Adam and Eve were expelled from Eden, God no longer could make His dwelling on the earth. Heaven was the only place suitable for His habitation. Mankind needed God to come back. And Jacob's ladder was God's way of saying He had a plan to answer that need.

The first expression of God reaching into the earth with His presence was in the tabernacle of Moses. God used this mobile sanctuary as His first Bethel. It was the one place in all of the earth where He chose to manifest the reality of His heavenly throne. The Israelites carried the tabernacle until it came to rest in the promised land. By God's command, King

Solomon constructed the temple in Jerusalem. All of Israel hoped that God's "Bethel" would enjoy a permanent home in Jerusalem. But what many of the Jewish people failed to see was that the temple pointed to a reality much greater than itself. The true temple or Bethel was God's Messiah.[6]

> Truly, truly, I say unto you, you will see heaven opened, and the angels of God ascending and descending on the Son of Man.
> —John 1:51

The coming of Messiah wasn't in a royal palace or in some immaculate temple with a spire that humans had erected to pierce the heavens. It happened without any pomp or official announcement from the state. A lowly stable in Bethlehem provided the cradle by which the humble-hearted God reached down to men. The insurmountable chasm that separated heaven and earth was bridged by the greatest gift of love: the incarnation of the Son of God. The ladder that Jacob had seen in the dream had come to Israel. The eternal God took on human flesh and the Messiah Jesus was born as the Bethel of God.

Jesus lived in sinless obedience to the Father and embodied perfect agreement with God as a man. His perfect life qualified Him to stand before God on behalf of sinful men. As the sole representative of mankind before God, Jesus bore the cross and absorbed the wrath of God for sin. The Righteous One stood before God on the behalf of the unrighteous. The Messiah's sinless life and atoning death provided the needed bridge for a rebellious world. Jesus Christ fulfilled God's sovereign plan. Through Jesus, the kingdom of heaven had come to earth through His intercession.

[6] Jn. 2:19–22.

From Genesis to Revelation, the Bible makes it clear that, since the fall, God has been breaking into our lost world through the ministry of intercession. Whatever redemptive move God has made to restore heaven and earth, He has made in partnership with human intercessors. God released His gracious mercy to the human race through one man, Noah. We also know that Abraham was the one man through whom God promised the coming Messiah, blessing all nations through His election of Israel. Even the entire temple system itself was based upon the ministry of the one high priest who stood before God on behalf of Israel. Yet all of these representatives pointed forward to the one Man who alone was worthy to stand before a holy God on behalf of sinful man as the perfect High Priest.[7] Christ is the ultimate intercessor and the fulfillment of a long line of intercessors who pointed to His perfect ministry.

The City of God

What is it about a city that is so important? In many ways, the Bible is the tale of two cities. On the one hand, we have Satan hell-bent on establishing Babylon as the world's capital, and on the other, God is executing an eternal plan to establish the New Jerusalem as the eternal city of the redeemed. A great city demonstrates power, glory, and allegiance. Obviously neither God nor the devil is merely interested in architectural engineering and city-planning councils. God wants people. And so does Satan. In both cases, the city becomes the community of their followers. Babylon consists of those who have been seduced by the devil's vision for mankind. And, as the Bride, the New Jerusalem is the community freed by the gospel of God, joined to Jesus Christ in faith.

[7] See the book of Hebrews.

Through the cross, God has set an inescapable plumb line for the entire human race. Faced with God's crucified Messiah, everyone must choose their citizenship. Those who refuse God's gospel remain citizens in a kingdom with a dark lord who enslaves his subjects to the work of sin and metes out wages of death in return for their labor. The king of this kingdom is leading his subjects to seek a city in this age that is free from their Creator, and he has no capacity for mercy towards those who oppose or obey him.

But those who renounce their citizenship of the kingdom of darkness and believe in the gospel of God inherit a citizenship of an entirely different order. In Christ, God has created a whole new race, a new creation (2 Cor. 5:17). All who repent of their allegiance to the king of Babylon and surrender their lives to the Lord Jesus Christ receive a new citizenship. We are strangers and foreigners in the earth because we have become citizens of the city of God.

Not only do we enjoy a new heavenly citizenship in Christ, but God has also taken up a new residence. Through the power of the Holy Spirit, the Church has become the Bethel of God. Christians are now the dwelling place of God in the earth. All who say yes to Jesus are joined with Him. Each human heart that believes the gospel becomes a "Bethlehem"; the glory of heaven breaks into earth as the Lord Jesus takes His throne in the life of a believer. Together the Church is the Body of Christ. We are now the living expression of Jesus in the world.

Ultimately the Bethel of God will be a city where God and man once again enjoy the perfect harmony of the original order. Jesus promised that He would not return until the "gospel of the kingdom of God [was] proclaimed throughout the whole world" (Mt. 24:14). When the Great

Commission is complete, Jesus will appear, and every knee in heaven and on earth shall bow. At long last, God's sovereign plan will be consummated as heaven is reunited with the earth at the second coming of Christ. The city of God will descend, unifying heaven and earth. All those who have been strangers in Babylon will at long last realize their true citizenship in the New Jerusalem.

FOUR
A RETURN TO THE TOWER

WITH THE OVERARCHING THEOLOGICAL CONCEPTS in place and the foundational strategies at work behind Babylon established, we can now revisit the original story of Babel with a deeper sense of understanding. The account of the Tower of Babel is a fascinating look into the infancy of Babylon. Arthur W. Pink reminds us: "The first mention of anything in scripture always calls for the most particular attention, inasmuch as the initial occurrence of any term or expression in the Word of God invariably defines its meaning and forecasts its subsequent significance and scope."[1] So with the biblical theology we have developed in mind, let's return to the story of Babel.

To help direct our study of Genesis 11, we'll use the eight characteristics of Babylon the Great from Revelation 17 and 18 as a template. It is important to keep in mind that the Tower of Babel is the first expression of what is fully revealed in the last chapters of Revelation. The evaluation of the Lord when He saw the city and Tower of Babel was that "this is only the beginning of what they will do" (Gen. 11:6).

[1]   Pink, *The Antichrist*, 234.

Mother of False Religion

The city and Tower of Babel was the birthplace of a satanic strategy to use a human city as a conduit for releasing demonic power into the earth. Building the tower wasn't just an opportunity for the people of Shinar to express their architectural ambitions; it was an attempt to reach into the spirit realm in allegiance with evil powers.

The Arabic name given to the Tower of Babel (*bab-ili*) means "gateway of the gods." This name betrays the satanic strategy at work in Babylon. To accomplish this evil objective, human partnership was required. There is little doubt that the Babelites had intended their tower to be a great temple. The Babelites were seduced into thinking that the sky was where the gods lived, and that building a tower reaching into heaven would be evidence of their rightful place among the gods. But the word "Babel" rendered in Hebrew sounds incredibly like the word *balal,* which means "confusion." The irony in these two meanings is inescapable. While the Babelites were totally confident that they were building a gateway to heaven, God deemed their religion utter spiritual confusion (*balal*). Confusion always accompanies disobedience.[2] When humans embrace spiritual lies and reject what light they have, they are left with nothing but the darkness of their own desires. The Babelites knew of God's command to fill the earth, and the rejection of it led to their delusion.[3]

The Spirit of Jezebel

It is interesting to note that the city of Babylon is repeatedly personified as a harlot queen in the Bible. Why is this? One cannot help but think about the infamous Jezebel in

2   Rom. 1:18–25; 2 Thes. 2:9–12.
3   Gen. 11:4.

connection with this portrait.[4] With her rule, she seduced the Israelites into the grossest forms of idolatry and immorality. Queen Jezebel was a seductive force propagating false religion and persecuting the true people of God.[5] The portrait of the woman Jezebel is the personification of Babylon. Like Jezebel, the spirit behind Babylon seduces people with compromise in order to establish her reign.

But long before the destructive nature of Jezebel was released in Israel, the earth groaned under the feet of another woman of unequaled political power and insidious influence—Semiramis. This enigmatic figure is attached to Nimrod in a way that history does not fully account for.[6] Because such mystery shrouds her, there is no way to identify exactly what she did, yet she looms over human history as the prototypical woman of great influence who seduces and manipulates her way to power. Dante wrote of her as among the lustful ones suffering in the hellfire of the inferno:

> Empress over lands of many tongues
> her vicious tastes had so corrupted her
> she licensed every form of lust with laws
> to cleanse the stain of scandal she had spread[7]

No clear historical account of Semiramis exists. The stories handed down often conflict regarding the events of her

---

[4] Jezebel was the pagan wife of Ahab, king of Israel. As queen, she used the king as a means to the throne. Ahab was king in name only; Jezebel became the real ruler in Israel. (See 1 Kgs. 16:31f.)

[5] See Part III for a fuller exposition of Jezebel and Babylon.

[6] Some accounts say that Semiramis was Nimrod's mother, while others say that she succeeded him and she was the founder of Babylon. Certain historians hold that Semiramis' son conspired against her to take power, and others that she conspired against Nimrod to take his place.

[7] Dante, *The Portable Dante,* 28.

life.[8] But if we lay aside the contradictory details for a moment and just consider the general caricature of the woman, a familiar portrait arises. According to the legend of Semiramis, an ancient Mesopotamian woman was a key figure in the establishment of Babylon. She possessed unmatched beauty and extreme political power. She was known to adorn herself in jewels of every kind and fully indulge in every luxury. She practiced and sanctioned the lewdest acts of sexual immorality.[9] She later became the high priestess of Babylonian idol worship.[10] Amazingly, this (extra-biblical) historical portrait of Semiramis is strikingly similar to the (biblical) personification of the city of Babylon.

According to legend, Semiramis was believed to have miraculously conceived a son named Tammuz who was considered a savior to his people. Babel was the birthplace of the first false Christ. The worship of Baal so often condemned in Scripture had its roots in this tradition. John Walvoord writes, "The doctrines of the mystery religions of Babylon seem to have permeated the ancient world, giving rise to countless mystery religions, each with its cult and individual beliefs offering a counterfeit religion and a counterfeit god in opposition to the true God revealed in the scriptures."[11] From apostate Christian belief to all-out paganism, all false religion has its roots in Babylon. Mormonism, pantheism, Kabala, Wicca, astrology, and every New Age belief have their beginning in Babylon. The religious delusion released at Babel has plagued humanity ever since.

---

[8]   "Such, then, are the conflicting accounts which may be found in the historians regarding the career of Semiramis." Diodorus Siculus, *Book II*, 20.

[9]   Ibid., 20.

[10] Walvoord, *The Revelation of Jesus Christ*, 247.

[11] Ibid, 248.

Enthroned upon the Nations

In the book of Revelation, the apostle John saw a great harlot seated upon the nations of the earth (Rev. 17:1, 15). This vision is a clear indication that Babylon the Great will arise in the end times with unequaled political power. But the global dominance that John foresaw was foreshadowed in the harlot city's very first manifestation at Babel.

Nimrod, king of Babylon, established several other cities in the region. The scope of his kingdom included Erech, Akkad, and the mighty Assyrian city of Nineveh.[12] When we consider the vast reach of King Nimrod, it becomes evident that he wasn't content with ruling the land of Shinar; his ambitious thirst was for global power. In Old Testament Hebrew thought, Assyria was so synonymous with Nimrod's conquests that the prophet Micah refers to the land of Assyria as "the land of Nimrod" (Mic. 5:6). Thousands of years before Hitler, Napoleon, Caesar, or Alexander, Genesis 10 gives a brief glimpse of the world's first dictator.

When Scripture records that Babel was the beginning of Nimrod's kingdom, it is not only speaking chronologically. Certainly Babel was the first place of Nimrod's rule, but it was also his power base.[13] Babel was Nimrod's political citadel and became the world's very first capital. Babel's early prominence is also reflected in the mythical Babylonian creation story, the *Enuma Elish*, in which Babylon is the center of the universe. While this is certainly a false account of creation, it shows how central Babylon was in the earliest records of human history.

[12] Gen. 10:8–10.

[13] Babylon had a supremacy over the other cities as the metropolis and royal residence; although it did not rise to the grand dimensions designed by its proud and impious founder." Augustine, *The City of God,* 628.

Center of Global Commerce

Located on the Euphrates River, the city was strate-gically situated to become the dominant trading place in the region. The river ports in Babel were frequented by all kinds of merchants and merchandise from around the land of Shinar. As the hub of commerce, Babel could fully access and utilize the abundant riches of the land. There were numerous settlements in the plain of Shinar, but all resources flowed to the single city of Babel.

The city and Tower of Babel were not the result of a primitive society of hunter-gatherers. Once settled in the fertile plain, they reaped the benefits of an agricultural and pastoral lifestyle, progressing beyond concern for day-to-day survival. No longer were they a disorganized mass of migrating people, but a unified society with time to de-vote themselves to advances in agriculture, architecture, and civil law. Babel grew from a settlement of wandering tribes to become the first bustling metropolis, the most advanced place on earth. This transformation took place over centuries, and culminated in a society bent on using their free time and abundant resources to consciously defy God's command.

A City United in Rebellion against God

Why was the building of Babel so egregious? At its core, the act was nothing less than blasphemy. In biblical language, a name has a much fuller and richer meaning than it does today—a name is the character or reputation by which one is known. When the builder of Babel declared, "Let us make a name for ourselves," what they were say-ing was, "Let's do something that will create a reputation that won't be forgotten." In pursuing human achievement and civil progress, the Babelites forgot the sovereign God who had created the beauty of heaven and earth for their enjoyment, the God who had spared their forefather Noah from the flood. In their growing delusion, they lost sight of the fact that God had designed them to magnify His name (reputation), not theirs.[14] Since the beginning, God has designed humans for the glory of His name. God built it into the fabric of human spiritual DNA to recognize and praise His greatness.[15]

Every human being is also wired for significance.[16] This innate desire is from God, and the Lord satisfies it in those who love Him. Satan understands that humans have this need for significance, and his temptations often come along these lines. The perverted desire for fame that litters popular culture today was present even in the earliest civilization. It was then, as it is today, satanically manipulated. This very desire for fame drove the effort to build Babel. Satan twisted the natural need for significance into a consuming pride that demanded recognition, with utter contempt for the glory of God.

It is difficult to imagine that just a few generations after God had flooded the entire earth, all of humanity would again be united in rebellion against Him. In Eden, the devil had planted seeds of mistrust and suspicion of God; over time those seeds grew into cedars of outright corporate rebellion against God.

[14] Piper, *The Pleasures of God*, 97f.

[15] God promises to gladly give a great name in return to those who choose to exalt His superior name. King David was obsessed with praising the name of God and making His name known in the earth. Because David lost himself in the magnification of the Lord's name, God in turn gave David a great name. David is now known throughout the earth as one of the greatest saints in history because, unlike the men of Babel, he sought to make a name for the Lord.

[16] Bickle, *The Pleasures of Loving God,* 117f.

She Intoxicates the Nations with Sexual Immorality

The luxury of city life brings many trappings—when the food source and supply chains were established in the land of Shinar, the people could do other things besides wonder where the next meal would come from. Over the decades, life in Shinar became less and less about survival and more about pleasure. It is no secret that luxury and sloth breed lasciviousness.[17]

Here we must again return to the influence of Semiramis. The ancient historian Diodorus Siculus writes of her, "In this place she passed a long time and enjoyed to the full every device that contributed to luxury ... choosing out the most handsome of the soldiers she consorted with them and then made away with all who had lain with her."[18] As quoted earlier from Dante, Semiramis was thought to have actually changed the civil laws of the land to justify her lewd practices; from these accounts, it seems Semiramis was so lascivious that she actually legislated lust.

When defiance against God is added to luxurious circumstances, it is certain that sexual immorality will be in the picture. One can only surmise the kinds of aberrant sexual behavior that the Babelites embraced under Semiramis' leadership. It's not clear how far this moral decay may have progressed, because it isn't explicitly mentioned in the text. But if we consider all the factors—Babel's economic prosperity, their spiritual rebellion recorded in the Bible, and the immorality mentioned by secular historians—we have solid grounds for concluding that the people of Babel gave way to sexual perversion on a corporate level.

---

[17] Even mighty King David succumbed to this reality in 2 Samuel 11:1–4.

[18] Diodorus Siculus, *Book II*, 393.

Persecution of the Saints

Throughout the Bible, God hides His people in strategic places.[19] When the mighty prophet Elijah fled from
Jezebel's persecution and cried out to God that he was
the only one who had not worshiped Baal, the Lord gen-
tly reminded him that there were 7,000 of God's people
who had not bowed their knee in idolatry.[20] Whether He
leaves one man or one thousand, it is God's nature to always preserve a people for Himself, even in the direst of
circumstances.

The exact role of God's people in Babel is not speci-
fied. But one thing is certain: they were involved in the
ministry of intercession. The people of God are bidirec-
tional intermediaries. They not only stood before their lost
neighbors on behalf of God, proclaiming a message of repentance; they also stood before God on behalf of their
lost neighbors, praying that God would mercifully intervene and bring the will of heaven to bear upon earth.

The Bible teaches that God is ever looking for those
who will stand in agreement with Him as He releases His
kingdom power in the earth.[21] The true spirit of intercession is standing in obedient agreement with God as the
Holy Spirit works to release the blessing of heaven on
those who would otherwise never experience it. God has
chosen to release His governmental will into the created
realm through the ministry of intercession.[22] To put it another

[19] For further arguments that God's people were present, see Augustine, *The City of God*, 624.

[20] 1 Kgs. 19.

[21] "For the eyes of the Lord run to and fro throughout the earth that He
may strongly support those whose heart is completely His" (2 Chr.
16:9, NASB).

[22] "Ask of me, and I will give you the nations your heritage, and the
ends of the earth for your possession" (Ps. 2:8).

way, the kingdom of heaven comes to earth through intercession. Or, as Andrew Murray puts it, "God rules the world through the prayer of the saints."[23]

The message and the lifestyle of the people of God made them strangers in Babel, alien to the ideology and values of Babel. This remnant of faithful believers would have needed to be extremely diligent to escape the decadent influence of their neighbors. Clearly their message and lifestyle would have been entirely contrary to the priorities of the Babelites and offensive to the developing cultural sensibilities. Nimrod would certainly have viewed any disloyalty as a threat to his agenda for Babel and would have dealt with offenders accordingly. Though there is no explicit biblical evidence for it, persecution in this context would have been likely.[24]

Staging Area for the Antichrist

> It is when people forget God that tyrants forge
> their chains.[25]
>
> —Patrick Henry

While the party in Babel raged on, a power was at work to bring every human soul into subjection to darkness. At the very same time the Babelites were indulging in every device and enjoying their apparent freedom from God, Nimrod was forging their chains.

The relationship between Babylon and the Antichrist is one of the darkest and strangest in the entire Bible. The apostle John sees it depicted in Revelation 17: "a woman

[23] Murray, "Fifth Lesson," *With Christ in the School of Prayer.*
[24] Pink concludes that Nimrod "relentlessly sought out and slew God's people." (*The Antichrist,* 222).
[25] Henry, *Liberty Tree.ca.*

sitting on a scarlet beast which was full of names of blasphemy…" (v. 3).

This vision is odd indeed. It depicts the great harlot
(Babylon) riding on the back of the beast (the end-time
empire of the Antichrist).[26] Babylon the Great will be the
capital city of the empire that will arise in the end times.
Ladd explains, "As the seat of godless civilization, the great
harlot has achieved her glory because she has been made
great by the beast and is completely dependent upon it."[27]
In the end times, the harlot city's seat of power will be atop
the Antichrist's empire.

Yet we see a surprising turn of events later in the very
same chapter when the "beast will hate the prostitute"
(Rev. 17:16). There is a complete reversal of the relationship between Babylon and the Antichrist. The harlot that is
riding on top of the beast in the beginning of Revelation 17
is a victim of the beast at the end of the chapter. The Bible
clearly declares that the Antichrist will demonstrate his authority over Babylon the Great by destroying the mighty
city with fire.

This prophetic picture illuminates the satanic strategy
at work. Babylon will flood the earth with sin to condition
the earth's inhabitants for the Antichrist's leadership. In the
end times, Babylon the Great will delude the nations and
prepare the earth for the greatest reign of terror in history.

In his account of the Tower of Babel, the Jewish historian Josephus shows that this reality was at work. He
writes:

> Now it was Nimrod who excited them to such
> an affront and contempt of God. He was the

26 See Chapter 2.
27 Ladd, *Revelation of John,* 223.

grandson of Ham, the son of Noah, a bold man, and of great strength of hand. He persuaded them not to ascribe to God as if it was through His means they were happy, but to believe that it was their own courage which procured that happiness. He also gradually changed the government into tyranny, seeing no other way of turning men from the fear of God, but to bring them into a constant dependence upon his power.[28]

Nimrod is the prototype of the Antichrist. His very name, "the rebel," accords with the apostle Paul's description of the Antichrist as "the man of lawlessness" (2 Thes. 2:3). As we have seen, Nimrod was driven to attain greater measures of power and glory, displayed in a global empire. In all likelihood he demanded the allegiance and adoration, if not worship, of his subjects.[29] According to Pink, "In Nimrod and his schemes we behold Satan's initial attempt to raise up a universal ruler of men. In his inordinate desire for fame, in the mighty power that he wielded, in his ruthless and brutal methods, in his blatant defiance of the Creator, in his founding of the kingdom of Babel . . . we cannot fail to see that we have a wonderfully complete typical picture of the person, the work, and the destruction of the Antichrist."[30]

As the eschatological city Babylon the Great will be empowered by the Antichrist but will ultimately pave the way for his totalitarian regime, so the same dynamic played

---

[28] Josephus, *Josephus: The Complete Works,* 40.

[29] "If the type [of Antichrist] be perfect, and we are fully assured it is so, then, as the Lawless One will yet do, Nimrod demanded and received *Divine honors.*" Pink, *The Antichrist,* 223.

[30] Ibid., 224.

out in the first generations after Noah's flood. According to Jewish tradition, Nimrod was the one who first inspired the people's imagination to build the Tower of Babel. He then acted to change the government into tyranny. The promise of human progress, human achievement, and human glory in the context of idolatry and sexual immorality served as the social conditioning needed to open the way for Nimrod to establish his reign.

Swift Judgment

When the apostle John foresaw the fall of Babylon the Great in the end times, he saw the kings of the earth lamenting the city's destruction, saying, "Alas! Alas! You great city, you mighty city, Babylon! For in a single hour your judgment has come" (Rev. 18:10).

In a single hour, Babylon the Great will go from sitting as a queen without equal to being cast down completely destitute. As Jezebel was thrown to her death from her lofty window (2 Kgs. 9:33), so the mighty power of Babylon will fall suddenly from great heights. At the end of the age, Babylon's ultimate fate will be utter and total destruction. Annihilation was not Babel's fate, however. Though God's assessment of the situation and execution of judgment came suddenly, He did not devastate the city. The Lord mercifully intervened before the city was able to mature in its wickedness. Had the city been left to its own devices, there is no telling the evils that Nimrod would have initiated and the divine judgment required to punish it. Instead, the kindness and wisdom of God in dealing with prideful men was fully displayed. Because the Lord had deemed their evil attempt to reach into the heavens confusion (*balal*), He translated their spiritual confusion into the confusion of their language.

The judgment of Babel is meant to cause us to pause—
to take a step back and meditate on the supremacy of
God. The story of the city and tower of Babel is not primarily about human rebellion or even Satan's scheme to dominate the world. Those elements are certainly involved, but
if we lose sight of the ultimate lesson of Babel, we will
do ourselves a great disservice. Primarily, it is about the
glory and supremacy of God. The city of Babylon demonstrates all the rebellion that devils and humans can muster
against God. The great city and skyscraper; the defiance
and idolatry; the mighty leader Nimrod and the campaign
to make a name for themselves—it all comes to nothing
when God determines to briefly demonstrate His absolute
supremacy.

The Babelites thought they could build a tower "whose
top is in the heavens." The Bible follows that statement
with "the Lord came down to see the city and the tower"
(Gen. 11:45). It was almost as if God couldn't stoop down
far enough to see the tower from His lofty place in heaven,
so He had to come down to see it.[31] Whether the Tower of Babel or the Burj Dubai,[32] the greatest architectural
achievements of man are but anthills before God.

Moving Forward

Satan will soon deceive the nations into joining together in one final attempt to build a global community free
from the "restraints" of the knowledge of God. The temptation of human achievement and progression will bait the
nations into building a city based upon a godless ideology.
It will be a scenario that will take the meager beginnings of

[31] Mathews, *NAC: Genesis 1–11:26*, 468.
[32] At the time of writing this book, the Burj Dubai is scheduled to be the
tallest freestanding building in the world.

Genesis 11 to a truly global scale. In the end times, Babylon the Great will arise as the religious, economic, and political capital of the world, exerting an incredible cultural influence on the nations. Serving as the nerve center of a global network of false religion, Babylon the Great will be the greatest conduit of demonic power in history, and will prepare the world for the Antichrist.

But that is only part of the story. This is the tale of two cities. The devil isn't the only supernatural agent working towards establishing a city in the earth. This is the timeless story of two opposing kings seeking to bring their kingdoms to earth. One city is a harlot that corrupts the earth with her influence; the other, a Bride prepared for eternal matrimony. All of human history bears the marks of this struggle. Everyone must choose their citizenship. The story begins in Babel and weaves its way through the Babylonian and Roman empires. Its legacy continues on today and will reach its climax in the end times.

We have taken the first step in understanding the history of Babylon and the people of God. But this is just the beginning. Thousands of years after Nimrod, Babylon will rise to dominate the earth once again.

PART II

THE BABYLONIAN EMPIRE

F I V E
NEO-BABYLON

THE YEARS FOLLOWING THE TOWER OF BABEL would turn to millennia before the harlot city returned to her seat of power. Thousands of years after Nimrod established the greatest city in the world, a new king would take up where he left off. A new chapter in the Babylon legacy was ready to be written. The demonic principality that had once seduced the human race to unlock the gateway of the gods was rising again, this time ascending to dominate the world in a much fuller measure than it had at Babel.

To track the development of the Babylon phenomenon, we must travel through the years when the land of Shinar became known as Babylonia, named after its chief city. Babel had suffered a major setback with the confusion of languages, but the proto-metropolis continued on. In spite of numerous invasions and persistent changes in government, it remained a major economic and cultural power in the Orient. Rulers drooled at the prospect of controlling the elusive city so that they might boast of having it as a jewel in their crown. For thousands of years, Babylon stood as the prize city of Mesopotamia.

Even when the brutal Assyrian Empire captured Babylon, the city remained in a constant state of revolt. Assyria's occupying force could not quell the continual insurgencies. The Babylonians had determined to win their independence and no amount of blood was counted too precious a price to pay for it. The city was nearly destroyed with fire in the battles that were fought to control her. The glory of Babylon's early days was swallowed by the devastation brought on by Assyria's heavy-handed tactics.

When at last the power of the Assyrian Empire began to wane, the native Chaldean tribe moved in to recover Babylon. This time they successfully held the city against the once-unstoppable Assyrian army, marking a victorious turning point. It was the twilight of Assyrian world domination and the dawning of the Chaldean dynasty. In 626 BC, Babylon came under Chaldean control and the stage was set for the next manifestation of the great harlot.

The ancient spirit of Babylon was stirring once again in the hearts of men. The time was near and the tide rising. It would not be long before a wave of spiritual delusion washed over the earth. Babylon was reemerging as the capital of the world. Her sins were being laid up—brick upon sinful brick—until the time when God would judge her blasphemous pride with a swift stroke of His right hand. But before the empire fell, the Lord would use it as a tool for His glory.

General Nebuchadnezzar

The Chaldean king, Nabopolassar, began the work of rebuilding Babylon after the destruction wreaked by the Assyrians. He had a lofty vision for his beloved city. Convinced that the gods had called him to make Babylon the greatest achievement in human history, Nabopolassar would not live to see the day when his city sat as queen of the earth. That unholy privilege was destined for his son, Nebuchadnezzar, crown prince of the Chaldeans and commander of the Babylonian army. Possessing unrivaled political and military genius, Nebuchadnezzar would take his father's vision for Babylon and impose it upon the world.

General Nebuchadnezzar was advancing on the reeling Assyrian army, but there was a greater threat to Babylon lurking in the shadows. Like a group of jackals hoping to scavenge the prey of an exhausted lion, the Egyptians were looking to fill the void left by the overwhelmed Assyrians. While Nebuchadnezzar's energy was spent dethroning the Assyrian Empire, Egypt was waiting to make its move.[1] At the news of Babylon's expanding military campaigns against Assyria, the Egyptians hoped to capitalize on the opportunity. The king of Egypt knew Nebuchadnezzar would have his hands full; he mobilized his forces and led an incursion into hostile territory. He moved north into an Assyrian province to capture the city of Carchemish on the Euphrates River. The small river-city served as a proficient base of operations against the Babylonians.

But any hope the Egyptians entertained of thwarting Nebuchadnezzar's expansion and retaining their influence in the west was futile. It was a year of divine destiny for the crown prince of Babylon; the kingdoms of the world were destined to fall into his hands. He led his forces in a surprise attack on Carchemish. The fighting was fierce and the slaughter heavy. The Babylonians met a battle-hardened, veteran force. Many of Nebuchadnezzar's men fell. But the severe bloodletting only seemed to make the

[1] Assyria continued to lose its hold on the region until its own capital, Nineveh, finally fell.

Babylonian army stronger. As the battle wore on, the Egyptian army weakened. Soon their famed forces were bolting in mass exodus. The battle was decisive. Nebuchadnezzar had thoroughly defeated the last remaining threat to Babylon's supremacy.

As the Egyptians poured out of the region in full retreat, the Babylonian army followed in relentless pursuit. Chasing the Egyptians through Syria, Nebuchadnezzar wanted to permanently cripple their military. But shocking news from Babylon would cut the chase short. Destroying the Egyptian army would have to wait. While still on the battlefield, Nebuchadnezzar received news of his father's death. With the victory over the Egyptian army secure and his enemy in flight, Nebuchadnezzar mounted his horse and sped across the desert to lay his claim to the throne.

The Coronation

As Nebuchadnezzar neared the city, he could hear the roar of the crowds awaiting his arrival. He was hailed by all as the hope and future of Babylon. Banners waved to his left and right. The streets of the city were lined with adoring subjects all shouting their undying allegiance to the new king. As Nebuchadnezzar neared the end of the elaborate parade, he could see his father's palace. He dismounted his royal horse and began to climb the steps where the prominent men of Babylon waited to crown him.[2]

Nebuchadnezzar stood to face the roaring crowds. He raised his hand and silence fell over all. He opened his mouth and gave a stirring speech that seemed to cast a spell over the masses. The people roared as he declared

---

[2] While there is no historical account of Nebuchadnezzar's coronation, Wiseman does briefly address it. Wiseman, *Nebuchadrezzar* [sic] *and Babylon*, 19.

that it was the will of the gods to make him king and promised that he would lead Babylon into a new era. The nobles and palace officials presented Nebuchadnezzar with the throne and crown of Babylon. The names of the Babylonian gods were invoked as the pagan priests blessed his kingship. On September 6, 605 BC, Nebuchadnezzar claimed the throne. The great military leader of the Chaldeans had entered the world stage as king of Babylon.

Nebuchadnezzar was well acquainted with the legends of Babylon; he loved the great city's ancient traditions. His father's passion for Babylon's destiny had captured his imagination from boyhood. The greatest of Nebuchadnezzar's deeply held religious convictions was his divine calling to make Babylon an earthly expression of heaven. His primary concern in military conquest was to rebuild the city in service to the gods, to finish what was started thousands of years before.[3]

To finance Nebuchadnezzar's plan for Babylon, the army marched through the Mesopotamian region virtually unopposed, exacting taxes and taking spoil. Any city refusing to submit to taxation chose a cruel fate. Nebuchadnezzar's forces were expert at siege warfare. The sieges could last for years.[4] Like a python squeezing the life out of its prey, once the Babylonians began a siege, it was only a matter of time. Resistance could not be sustained for long.

Once conquered, a city's wealth became the possession of the empire. Everything in the city was subject to being sent back to Babylon. Human spoil was considered part and parcel of the conquered city's treasures. The

---

[3] Nebuchadnezzar's radical ambitions would cause him to be remembered as the "Great Builder" of Babylon.

[4] Tyre and Sidon fell to Babylonian sieges; Lebanon's mighty cedar forests were used to build Babylonian temples and palaces.

plunder included politicians, soldiers, and craftsmen. The greatest treasures and human resources of the world were ransacked to build Babylon into a fantastical city of magnificent buildings and cutting-edge architecture.[5]

The Unfinished Tower

Nebuchadnezzar's visionary leadership made Babylon the greatest spectacle on earth, but his ambitions went far beyond the physical beauty of the city. Like his father, Nebuchadnezzar was deeply devoted to the will of the gods. And there was one calling of the gods greater than all others: to restore the ancient temple-tower that had stood in the city for thousands of years. Nebuchadnezzar's father had been obsessed with completing it. He was driven by the gods day and night, yet with all of his effort he was unable to finish it before his death.

As the new king of Babylon, Nebuchadnezzar would finish what his father had started. He focused every resource of the empire towards this historic project. For years the greatest architects and craftsmen of Babylon were devoted to it. The sky-high structure could be seen from anywhere in the city. Construction crews streamed up its stairs in a tireless effort to bring the needed materials. Every day the monstrous tower grew brick by brick.[6]

There was but one final addition to crown the project. At the top of the tower, Nebuchadnezzar built a temple for the gods to descend for intercourse with mankind.[7]

This exalted temple bridged the human realm with the

---

[5] Hundreds of years later, the ancient Greeks regarded the famous hanging gardens of Nebuchadnezzar's palace as one of the Seven Wonders of the World.

[6] The tower was made up of over 17 million bricks.

[7] Marshall, Millard, Packer, and Wiseman, *New Bible Dictionary*, 109.

realm of the gods. When it was finished, Nebuchadnezzar wrote his royal inscription:

> I MADE IT THE WONDER OF THE PEOPLE OF
> THE WORLD, I RAISED ITS TOP TO HEAVEN,
> MADE DOORS FOR THE GATES, AND I COV-
> ERED IT WITH BITUMEN AND BRICKS.[8]

The temple was the central feature of the city, the symbol of Babylon. For over two millennia, the ancient tower had been left half-built. Previous civilizations had tried to finish it, only to fail. Where Nimrod fell short, Nebuchadnezzar succeeded. The king of Babylon had completed the unfinished Tower of Babel.

Life in Babylon

Like a dark wave, sorcery swept over the empire. From military commanders and officers of state to the commoner, ascertaining demonic information was part of daily life in Babylon. Those who practiced the dark arts the most were given the positions of greatest influence. All the men of the royal court were experts in divination and astrology. No major political decision was made without first consulting the diviners. Discerning the will of demonic spirits by divination was woven into the fabric of Babylonian society.[9]

In Babylon, there was no separation between religion and economics. Her networks of pagan temples were the arteries through which the world's financial bloodstream pumped. The bulk of taxes gained by the Babylonian military campaigns were apportioned to feed the idolatrous

---

[8] Nebuchadnezzar's royal inscription was found by Robert Koldewey during an excavation in 1917. The stele is now part of the Schoyen Collection, MS 2063.

[9] Oates, *Babylon*, 128.

expansion. From agricultural trade to the booming industry of cult sacrifices, Babylon's temple system reaped huge profits from the greatest economy the world had ever produced.[10]

The middle class shriveled as pagan priests inundated Babylonian aristocracy. Temple leaders owned the trading centers in and around Babylon. Once the wealth of Babylon was in their avaricious grip, the temples began to double as lending centers. The interest gained from borrowing created even greater streams of revenue with which to "serve the gods." The average Babylonian's salary was so insignificant that long-term borrowing was expected.[11] The commoner was steeped in debt while the wealthy priests were profiting hand-over-fist, benefiting from ever-compounding interest. Pedaling lies and propagating spiritual darkness was big business in Babylon.

The network of false religion not only spread its tentacles into every aspect of commerce in Babylon, it established sexual immorality as a cultural way of life. The pagan beliefs and practices of the city made the atmosphere of Babylon ripe with lust. Babylon turned fornication into temple ritual as every woman of Babylon paid duty to the sex goddess by having intercourse with a stranger at least once in her life.[12] The corruption of the temple network immersed the citizens of Babylon into sexual immorality.

Babylon's power increased over the region as Nebuchadnezzar lived out his ambitions for world domination. The cities of Nineveh and Damascus were already under his control. The superiority of his army propelled him westward. With an unbending appetite for power, the king of Babylon

[10] Roux, *Ancient Iraq*, 401.
[11] Ibid., 403.
[12] Herodotus, *The Histories, Book I*, 199.

turned his malice on the kingdom of Judah and the people of God. The shadow of Babylon's influence had already covered all of Mesopotamia. Now the storm clouds began to gather over Jerusalem.

The Jerusalem Campaign

Nebuchadnezzar had heard of the Hebrews and their God many times. Stories and legends had reached his court of the mighty acts that their God had done for them. He was well aware of the devastating defeat Assyria had suffered and the mysterious massacre of their mightiest men when they had laid siege to Jerusalem (2 Kgs. 19:35). Still, his lust for power would not be deterred by such outrageous stories, for he had also heard of the renowned wealth of Solomon's temple. To conquer Jerusalem was to capture the greatest concentration of riches in the region. He determined to defeat the Hebrews and make the people of God subjects of his empire.

Nebuchadnezzar gathered his forces and made an expedition into the promised land. The full strength of Babylon's military might was demonstrated as they marched freely through Judah. Messengers were sent to Jerusalem demanding that the king of Judah pay tribute. When his demand was refused, Nebuchadnezzar followed his first message with another: "Prepare for war!"

The words echoed in King Jehoiakim's mind. In a moment, a flood of images filled his thoughts. No nation could stand against Nebuchadnezzar. Those who had tried were thoroughly defeated and their cities ransacked. Jehoiakim had heard the brutal stories of how Tyre and Sidon had already fallen to the Babylonian ruler. The idea of a war with Babylon melted the king's courage. King Jehoiakim quickly ordered a large sum from the national treasury to be brought before Nebuchadnezzar. Along with Jehoiakim's tribute came the subjugation of Jerusalem to Babylon.

It had been an extraordinary year for the king of Babylon. Not only had he driven the Egyptian army out of the region and claimed the throne of Babylon, but he had also accomplished something no one had ever done before. In 605 BC, Nebuchadnezzar brought the elusive city of Jerusalem under his control with nothing more than the threat of war. Like other cities he conquered, Nebuchadnezzar plundered the human spoil of Jerusalem and sent it back to Babylon. Among the exiled Jews was a young prophet named Daniel.

Jerusalem became another satellite in the harlot's growing network of cities. Year after year, the empire required enormous sums of money from Jerusalem's treasury. Just when the Jews thought the taxation could not get worse, rumors began to grow of Nebuchadnezzar's involvement with the Egyptians. His campaigns had driven him far from home. Was his army spread too thinly?

After consulting his advisors, the king of Judah decided that it was time to take a stand. The next time the small company of Babylonians came to Jerusalem to collect taxes, King Jehoiakim did not allow them into the city. Hoping that Nebuchadnezzar would be too busy with the Egyptians to bother with his small nation, Jehoiakim turned the Babylonians back. But Nebuchadnezzar wouldn't take no for an answer. The wealth of Jerusalem was far too lucrative to overlook. King Jehoiakim's refusal brought the Babylonian army and Nebuchadnezzar himself to Jerusalem's doorstep.

The approaching Babylonian army struck fear in Jehoiakim's heart. He had never dreamed that Nebuchadnezzar would act so quickly. The threat of his capital city under siege quickly caused King Jehoiakim to reconsider his decision. While still outside the city gates, Nebuchadnezzar offered terms of peace. He promised that if he were allowed into Jerusalem, no harm would come to any of the Jewish people. This was Jehoiakim's last chance to avoid certain disaster. Looking for any way of escape, King Jehoiakim quickly agreed to Nebuchadnezzar's terms and accepted the covenant of peace. With the full assurance of Nebuchadnezzar's peaceful intentions now in writing, Jehoiakim opened Jerusalem's gates to the king of Babylon.

Jehoiakim's royal court awaited Nebuchadnezzar on bended knee in a full demonstration of submission. The king of Babylon rode into Jerusalem as the crowds bowed in silence before him. Jehoiakim nervously extended a peaceful gesture, hoping for mercy. In his royal armor, Nebuchadnezzar dismounted and approached Jehoiakim. With a scowl, he gave his commanders a nod. They drew their swords and immediately put Jehoiakim to death, along with a number of the highest-ranking officials in Jerusalem.[13]

Nebuchadnezzar had neither regard for nor the remotest fear of the Jewish God. The Jews were his subjects, considered useful only in their service for Babylon. With Nebuchadnezzar's tentacles wrapped around the little nation, Judah's autonomy had never been so compromised. The king of Babylon did as he pleased with Judah. In 597, he exiled some 10,000 Jews of the highest ranks; Ezekiel the prophet, Jewish nobles, officers, and skilled craftsmen were all exiled to Babylonia.

[13] Josephus, The Complete Works, 326: In the spirit of the Antichrist, Nebuchadnezzar cared nothing for the covenant of peace he had mediated with Judah. Daniel 9:27 foretells the agreement the Antichrist will make with Israel, an agreement that he will later break. See Miller, NAC: Daniel, 271.

The Final Act of Defiance

After being installed by Nebuchadnezzar, the new king of Judah was nothing more than Babylon's puppet. King Zedekiah could live with it at first; he had no choice. But soon resentment began to grow in his heart. The only ones who despised King Zedekiah more than the Babylonians were his own people. Zedekiah would have been the laughingstock of Judah had the situation not been so dire. Privately his advisors began to entertain the idea that the nation should take a stand against Nebuchadnezzar. The king's spiritual advisors also backed the seditious advice. Prophet after prophet promised that God would surely bless any such attempt to break free from the pagan power of Babylon.

After years of submitting to Babylonian control and taxation, King Zedekiah decided to turn to Egypt for help. Though Nebuchadnezzar had soundly defeated the Egyptian army at Carchemish, Egypt had remained an independent nation, free from Babylonian rule. Over the years Egypt had led an anti-Babylonian coalition of nations to counter the power of Nebuchadnezzar's empire. King Zedekiah saw his opportunity to throw off the yoke of Babylon and joined the coalition.

When the news of Zedekiah's uprising reached Nebuchadnezzar's court, the full fury of Babylon was unleashed. The king of Babylon vowed that this would be the last time Jerusalem would be allowed to defy his empire. Nebuchadnezzar gathered his forces and marched his troops through the heartland of Judah. Stronghold after stronghold fell to the overwhelming force of the vast Babylonian army. Many of the towns and cities of Judah were flattened; the Jewish military defense was but a sandcastle before a tidal wave of pagan troops. After clearing the approach, the crimson tide of the Babylonian army flowed to the gates of Jerusalem under the direct command of Nebuchadnezzar.

The Babylonians dug in, knowing that the nearly impregnable walls of the city would take months if not years to penetrate. This time Nebuchadnezzar would offer no terms of peace. The latest advances in siege warfare were implemented. Siege walls and towers were built like a noose around Jerusalem to cut off all entrances and exits to and from the city. The hopes of Egyptian assistance to rescue the Jewish people faded as the Egyptian army proved no match for Nebuchadnezzar's forces. Jerusalem was completely surrounded.

SIX

THE FALL OF JERUSALEM

WHILE BABYLON WAS RISING to ever-increasing global political and economic power under Nebuchadnezzar's leadership, Jerusalem remained the true epicenter of the earth from heaven's perspective. Babylon was reclaiming its place as the center of every facet of human affairs, but heaven's focus was on an entirely different place. The Lord had chosen one nation through which to reveal Himself to the world.

The descendants of Abraham, Isaac, and Jacob were the objects of God's sovereign choice, and it was through this small nation that He was bringing the kingdom of heaven to earth. God's presence and glory were breaking into the earth through a single point. The dwelling place of God was not to be found in any of the immaculate architecture of Babylon. It was happening in the Jewish capital. The point of contact between heaven and earth—the place where the royal court and throne room of heaven found their earthly expression—was in the temple.

God's presence in the Jewish temple was so holy that only one man could enter the holiest place, and only once each year. A single high priest would enter God's throne room to make intercession for the people. Standing in the gap between a holy God and a sinful nation, the high priest offered the blood of sacrifice prescribed in the Law given to Moses. God's holy presence and heavenly glory was the most precious, unspeakable reality of the entire universe. Through the Law and the temple, He brought Himself to the realm of men.

The Kingdom of Judah

During Babylon's ascent, the Jewish kingdom of Judah was experiencing great civic and spiritual decline. Though they had recently enjoyed a great spiritual revival under King Josiah, who had faithfully led the nation back into the path of righteous living, his sweeping reforms weren't enough to deter future generations from turning from the Lord. After King Josiah had fallen in battle and his legacy was forsaken, the people of Judah quickly fell back into the vile sins of their forefathers.

Abandoning God had its consequences. The cold, stinging wind of sin was numbing the national conscience. The leaders of Judah were entirely oblivious to the spiritual darkness permeating their kingdom. They were confident that God was perfectly happy with His chosen nation. After all, they were the people of God. They had the Law of Moses. God was being worshiped in the temple. The problem wasn't sin, they told themselves. The problem was with the naysayers—those whose extremist view of God was detrimental to national interests. When confronted by God's prophets with the urgent need for national repentance, the leaders of Jerusalem indignantly asked, "What is our sin?" (Jer. 16:10). No message or messenger could penetrate their spiritual obstinacy. Yet God spoke plainly to them through servants like the prophet Jeremiah.

> Because your fathers have forsaken me, de-
> clares the Lord, and have gone after other gods
> and have served and worshiped them, and have
> forsaken me and have not kept my law, and be-
> cause you have done worse than your fathers,
> for behold, every one of you follows his stub-
> born, evil will, refusing to listen to me. Therefore
> I will hurl you out of this land into a land that
> neither you nor your fathers have known, and
> there you shall serve other gods day and night,
> for I will show you no favor.
> —Jeremiah 16:11–12

The spiritual leaders of Judah were leading the people astray from God's heart. The ever-persistent practice of idolatry was reaching new heights. The business leaders of Judah were exploiting the poor. The people of God, who were to be His praise in the earth, grew callous toward Him and neglected His law. God and His glory were disregarded, His beauty forsaken. The ones God had chosen to declare His name and to be a light to the nations were instead bringing reproach to His name as they pursued their own carnal ways. The leaders of Jerusalem seduced God's people into playing the harlot.

The Intercessors

The spiritual condition of the nation was bleak, but there was still hope. This was the same merciful God who promised Abraham that He would spare Sodom if ten righteous men could be found. The blow of God's righteous judgment over the nation could be softened if the Lord found humans to partner with Him and stand in the place of intercession.[1] Judah's spiritual condition was dark, but what made matters far worse, and ultimately sealed Jerusalem's fate, was that which the prophet Ezekiel spoke of:

> The people of the land have practiced extortion
> and committed robbery. They have oppressed
> the poor and needy, and have extorted from
> the sojourner without justice. And I sought for a
> man among them who should build up the wall
> and stand in the breach before me for the land,
> that I should not destroy it, but I found none.
>
> —Ezekiel 22:29–30

No one was standing in the place of intercession; no one cried out for God's power and mercy to come. It was bad enough that the royal descendants of King David had discarded the godly legacy left to them. But the priesthood too? It was true. Even the ones who were to function as the designated national intercessors had lost their way in the religious ritual and public recognition of their exalted positions. Ever since the garden of Eden, God's activity had been in partnership with humans. Now, with the ministry of intercession abandoned, there was no way to avert or minimize the coming judgment.

The Word of the Lord

God had given His people numerous warnings through the prophets. His judgment was now imminent in light of the wholesale moral decay, belligerent idolatry, and prevailing injustice that worsened by the day. Judah would not hearken to God's prophetic voices, nor did they learn from the destruction suffered by the northern kingdom just

[1]   Judgment might have been averted altogether if the nation had repented (Jer. 18:7–8).

a century before at the merciless hands of the Assyrians. Without an alternative more merciful to His people and faithful to His name, the heavenly decree for the destruction of Jerusalem was issued.

God's judgment on Judah came in a way that no religious Jew could have imagined. He used a pagan king as His rod of chastisement,[2] for it would be by the hand of a prideful and blasphemous Nebuchadnezzar that Jerusalem would fall. The man who would ultimately become an object of God's wrath would first be the Lord's chosen instrument to deal decisively with His people. God's people had given themselves over to spiritual harlotry; now He would give them over to the great harlot.

This unthinkable judgment was revealed to the prophet Habakkuk after he cried out concerning the increasing depths of Judah's depravity. God replied to Habakkuk in a way that even the faithful prophet had difficulty understanding: He would use His servant Babylon to discipline His people.

> Look among the nations, and see; wonder and be astounded. For I am doing a work in your days that you would not believe if told. For behold, I am raising up the Chaldeans, that bitter and hasty nation, who march through the breadth of the earth, to seize dwellings not their own. They are dreaded and fearsome; their justice and dignity go forth from themselves. Their horses are swifter than leopards, more fierce than the evening wolves; their horsemen press proudly on. Their horsemen come from afar;

[2] "Now I have given all these lands into the hand of Nebuchadnezzar, the king of Babylon, my servant" (Jer. 27:6).

they fly like an eagle swift to devour. They all come for violence, all their faces forward. They gather captives like sand. At kings they scoff, and at rulers they laugh. They laugh at every fortress, for they pile up earth and take it. Then they sweep by like the wind and go on, guilty men, whose own might is their god!

—Habakkuk 1:5–11

The Siege

King Zedekiah had defied mighty Nebuchadnezzar and would now taste his fury. The full might of Babylon had been brought to bear on a single objective—to conquer Jerusalem, the capital of Judah. The mighty walls of the city would not be penetrated easily, but the Babylonians utilized their most advanced siege-works and dug in, ready to stay for months. There was no escape.

With God's heavenly decree given for the destruction of Jerusalem, His prophets began to raise their voices to the leadership in Judah. God's greatest witness in Jerusalem during those dark days was the prophet Jeremiah. Jeremiah had remained in Jerusalem while others like Ezekiel and Daniel had already been taken to Babylonia in the earlier exiles. Jeremiah courageously carried a message that was fiercely resisted by the leadership of Judah. Despite the danger, he relentlessly warned King Zedekiah of God's decree to destroy the city of Jerusalem and deliver its citizens into captivity.

The siege wore on, the months elapsed into a year, and still the Babylonians were just outside the city wall, tightening their grip. Every day the tension grew as the citizenry of Jerusalem witnessed the embankments growing ever closer to the city walls. Jeremiah's message to King

Zedekiah was urgent but simple: the only way to minimize God's judgment by the hand of Nebuchadnezzar was to surrender to it. The Lord gave His people the choice; resist Nebuchadnezzar and be destroyed, or surrender to Babylon and minimize the judgment. Captivity in Babylon was inevitable for God's people; it was the next season decreed for them, and it could not be averted (Jer. 25:11).

Prophetic Voices

But King Zedekiah had other voices in his royal court. His closest advisors constantly reminded him what had happened the last time Nebuchadnezzar was welcomed into the city. Zedekiah wasn't willing to take that risk. He surrounded himself with a company of prophets who promised that God would soon supernaturally intervene to overthrow the Babylonians. They all quoted the scriptures and with dramatic gestures loudly proclaimed God's promises to act on behalf of His people.

Only one voice dissented: the prophet Jeremiah. When Zedekiah's men came to Jeremiah, hoping that Jeremiah would come to his senses and join the chorus of the other prophets and declare how God would deliver Jerusalem from Nebuchadnezzar's hand, Jeremiah prophesied:

> Thus says the LORD, the God of Israel: Behold, I will turn back the weapons of war that are in your hands and with which you are fighting against the king of Babylon and against the Chaldeans who are besieging you outside the walls. And I will bring them together into the midst of this city. I myself will fight against you with outstretched hand and strong arm, in anger and in fury and in great wrath ... I will give

Zedekiah king of Judah and his servants and the
people in this city who survive the pestilence,
sword, and famine into the hand of Nebuchadnezzar king of Babylon.

—Jeremiah 21:4–7

Deep down, King Zedekiah was haunted by the truth
of Jeremiah's message. But under the pressure of his
advisors, he chose to embrace the message of the false
prophets instead. The king did everything in his power to
silence Jeremiah and strengthen the people's resolve to
defy Nebuchadnezzar's siege. The corrupt spiritual and
political leadership of Judah supported Zedekiah in his decision to not simply ignore the prophecies of Jeremiah but
to persecute the faithful prophet as a treacherous Babylonian loyalist.[3]

Midnight in Jerusalem

A scourge of death springing from famine and disease
began to break out within the city. The choice to reject
God's message was becoming more deadly by the day.
To the inhabitants of Jerusalem, the only thing more frightening than dying from hunger and disease was the prospect of allowing Nebuchadnezzar into the city. Fear and
panic mounted as it became evident that the siege would
not lift before they had all perished of hunger or disease.
Zedekiah's control over the population began to slip. The
propaganda of the false prophets no longer brought comfort to the horrified citizens. Desperation grew to frenzy
under the growing pressure of starvation and the stench
and disease of the dead. During the chaos of those days,
the Babylonian forces broke through the wall. The dam

[3] Jeremiah was imprisoned for proclaiming the Word of the Lord (Jer.
38).

finally crumbled and the sea of pagan troops flooded into Jerusalem; after eighteen long months, the siege was over (Jer. 39:1).

All was lost. Realizing his reign was finished, Zedekiah took his family and escaped from Jerusalem through a secret tunnel. With Babylonian troops securing the chaotic city, Nebuchadnezzar entered Jerusalem, ordering his top commanders to capture Zedekiah. Interrogations quickly determined his whereabouts and King Zedekiah was overtaken in the plains of Jericho. He was brought before Nebuchadnezzar and, as expected, he received no mercy. Nebuchadnezzar slaughtered his family before him and ordered that Zedekiah's eyes be plucked out to make sure his murdered family would be the last image he ever saw.

Just as Jeremiah had prophesied, the citizens of Jerusalem who had survived the horrors of the siege were gathered and ordered to Babylon. The city was razed to the ground. The temple was pillaged and its treasures brought back to Babylon. The place of God's glory and presence in the earth was looted and burned. The kingdom of Judah was now fully under the pagan power of Nebuchadnezzar. In the year 586 BC, the destruction of the temple and the final exile were complete. The city of God had been turned into a heap of ash and the people of God were taken away. The Babylonian captivity would be in effect and the temple would not be rebuilt for seventy years. Though a remnant Jewish population was left in the city, most of the exiled Jews of that generation would not live to see Jerusalem again.

SEVEN

BABYLONIAN CAPTIVITY

> Look and see if there is any sorrow like my sorrow, which was brought upon me, which the LORD inflicted on the day of His fierce anger.
>
> —Lamentations 1:12

THE EERIE SOUNDS OF WEEPING and lament hung over the line of thousands that streamed eastward. Unimaginable dejection took hold of the Jewish people as they were led on a forced march out of the promised land. Exiled to a strange land of strange gods, the chosen people of God had lost their nation, their land, their city, their temple; they had been stripped of everything they held most dear, except for their God. Little did they imagine that yet another battle awaited them—a battle not for their bodies, but for their hearts and minds.

Stories of Babylonian architecture, science, idolatry, decadence, and luxury had drifted to Jerusalem over the years, but were thought to be exaggerations. All that the exiles had heard about the great city did not prepare them for what they found as they entered through the tall city gates, elaborately embellished with pagan images of dragons and bulls. From the time God's people entered Babylon until the day they left, they would be surrounded by the values, culture, and seductive power of the city.

> Thus says the LORD of hosts, the God of Israel, to all the exiles whom I have sent into exile from Jerusalem to Babylon: Build houses and live in them; plant gardens and eat their produce. Take wives and have sons and daughters ... seek the welfare of the city where I have sent you into exile, and pray to the LORD on its behalf, for in its welfare you will find your welfare.
> —Jeremiah 29:4–7

The city that was named for its defiant desire to reach into the realm of demons was to be subverted with prayer. God had promised that the power of heaven would be brought to bear on the affairs of Babylon as His people interceded on the city's behalf. The Lord's message to His broken people while they were in Babylon was two-fold: embrace the season of discipline, and open the gateway of heaven by way of intercessory prayer. God decreed a captivity that would last for seventy years. Nothing could be done to alter it. Many would live out the rest of their days in a pagan city far from the place they used to call home. They were to embrace their new city and overcome through prayer.

God's purpose to bring heaven's light to Babylon was only to be overshadowed by His purpose to spiritually refine His people through their captivity. Babylon was the only remedy for the spiritual illness that plagued Judah. Prayerlessness and dullness would be expelled from their hearts by their total immersion in Babylon. God was seeking sold-out worshipers who fully desired Him; He was going to use Babylon to drive them into wholehearted consecration.

> I will regard as good the exiles from Judah, whom I have sent away from [Jerusalem] to the land of the Chaldeans. I will set my eyes on them for good, and I will bring them back to this land. I will build them up, and not tear them down; I will plant them and not uproot them. I will give them a heart to know that I am the LORD, and they shall be my people and I will be their God, for they shall return to me with their whole heart.
> —Jeremiah 24:5–7

> When the seventy years are completed for Babylon, I will visit you, and I will fulfill to you my promise and bring you back to [Jerusalem] … Then you will call upon me and come and pray to me, and I will hear you. You will seek me and find me, when you seek me with all your heart.
> —Jeremiah 29:10, 12–13

The Fog of Prosperity

As the people settled in the Jewish ghettos of the great city of Babylon along the Chebar River, their fears of enslavement and oppression were eased. They discovered that their captivity would be nowhere near as brutal as the enslavement their ancient forefathers had endured in Egypt. In fact, the luxuries and freedoms of Babylon actually benefited the Jewish people in many ways. Most of the exiles purchased their own homes; some even started businesses. The religious tolerance of Babylon meant that the Jewish people were free to meet together to worship the Lord and read the Torah. The very first synagogues arose in Babylon. Jews could choose the occupations they wanted, as long as it served the purposes of the city and empire. Some even found life-long careers helping to engineer and build the exotic city. The people of God were found at every social level in Babylon. In situations ranging from Nebuchadnezzar's royal court to small street businesses, many of the exiled Jews actually grew rich during their stay.

But in all of their prosperity, many of the Jewish people lost sight of the demonic reality behind the city; they didn't realize that there was a satanic strategy at work to seduce them to compromise. The seduction was subtle but powerful. Every day the images, ideas, and lifestyle of Babylon barraged the heart and mind. In the midst of the Babylonian captivity, many Israelites began to lose their vision and destiny as the people of God. For many Jews, the luxury and excitement of the lifestyle in Babylon proved too much to resist. They fell in love with the spirit and splendor of the city, becoming oblivious to the spiritual delusion surrounding them. They came to love the luxury, the decadence. Liberal ideas about God were taught in many synagogues to justify the growing spiritual compromise. Not only were these Jews in Babylon; Babylon was finding its place in them.

But God was not through with Jerusalem. Even though the temple lay in ruins and the people of God had been exiled, God had promised that the house of prayer would be rebuilt.[1] The captivity would not last forever. Babylon was temporary; the pagan city was never meant to be a permanent home. The day would come when God would be finished with Babylon and call His people back to Jerusalem

[1]   Jesus referred to the temple in Jerusalem as the house of prayer (Mt. 21:13). See Isaiah 56:7 for an Old Testament example.

to rebuild the temple. But as the years of captivity wore on, it became apparent that many of the Jewish people would not return home, choosing to forsake God's purpose for Jerusalem in favor of citizenship in Babylon.

Daniel

Though many lost their hearts in Babylon, not everyone abandoned their spiritual moorings while in exile. God's faithful servants battled against the influence of Babylon. With weak but sincere effort to love God and keep their hearts for Him alone, a generation of faithful leaders and wholehearted worshipers came forth from the fires of Babylonian exile. As God had intended, Babylon refined the faithful. Among that company was the prophet Daniel and his compatriots.

In an attempt to assimilate other countries into the culture of Babylon, Nebuchadnezzar imported to his court the nobility of those he conquered so that they would be fully educated in Babylonian ways. Of the conquered Jews, the prophet Daniel and three other young men born of Jewish nobility were brought into Nebuchadnezzar's palace, where they were to be instructed in the arts and learning of Babylon.

To overcome the lure of Babylon, Daniel and his friends embraced a focused life. The devil wanted these young men, but they would not compromise. To escape the constant advances, they pursued one hundred percent obedience to God. The images of Babylon were a perennial threat. From the prostituted women walking the streets to the public sex rituals of the temples, the young men had to be diligent to reject these carnal indulgences. Their spiritual campaign to resist the compromise of Babylon began in the privacy of their hearts. Whether or not anyone was watching, they refused to embrace the luxuries and trappings of Babylon.

When the teenage men were ordered into the king's court, they gained access to the most exclusive privileges in all of Babylon. They could eat anything from the king's table; the most delicious of all kinds of food were readily available, cooked by the best chefs in the land, paired with the finest wines in the world. The delicious living was tempting. But with every kind of delicacy at their fingertips, they swam against the carnal tide, embracing instead a lifestyle of fasting. In refusing the delicacies of Babylon they were exercising a spiritual muscle that would be necessary for their spiritual survival in pagan surroundings.

While other exiles were lulled into apathy by life in Babylon, the four who were most greatly exposed to the temptations, luxury, and excess of the royal court overcame Babylon's enticements by embracing a radical lifestyle of fasting and prayer. Their hearts were not simply kept intact; as Daniel set his face toward God, the fire of his devotion actually increased. Resisting the temptations of Babylon and pursuing wholehearted obedience to God sharpened Daniel's spirit to a razor's edge.

The Image of the Beast

There were ominous indications that the Babylonian policy of religious tolerance was only an illusion. The religious freedoms of Babylon were as shaky as Nebuchadnezzar's blasphemous whims. The antichrist spirit would soon grip Nebuchadnezzar's heart in greater power than ever before. Satan's next attempt to cause the people of God to compromise would threaten their very lives. Daniel's friends had refused to be enticed with the pleasures of Babylon in private, but soon they would be faced with the pressure to bow under the public command of a tyrant.

For months Nebuchadnezzar concentrated his building efforts on a single project erected in the plain of Dura outside of the city. Government officials from every province of Babylonia were gathered for the dedication ceremony. When the king's officials assembled, they saw Nebuchadnezzar enthroned above the masses, displayed in all the pomp and splendor of Babylon. Crimson and black banners snapped in the wind over the people, keeping time with the court's most skillful musicians. The swell of music was majestic; the king's face intense. Every eye would have been fixed on him if something in the center of the crowd had not overshadowed all else. An enormous image towered ninety feet above them. It was a monstrosity of gold, different from all the other idols of the gods proliferating Babylon. It was the image of Nebuchadnezzar himself.[2]

The officials of Babylonia stared in wonder; the music died down. When silence had overtaken the crowds Nebuchadnezzar's herald spoke in a loud voice that echoed across the plain.

> You are commanded, O peoples, nations, and languages, that when you hear the sound of the horn, pipe, lyre, trigon, harp, bagpipe, and every kind of music, you are to fall down and worship the golden image that King Nebuchadnezzar has set up. And whoever does not fall down and

---

[2] For reasons why Nebuchadnezzar's image signified the king of Babylon, see Driver, *The Book of Daniel,* 35. See also Pink, *The Antichrist,* 230.

worship shall immediately be cast into a burning fiery furnace.

—Daniel 3:4–6

Never before had worship of any kind been a legal requirement in Babylon. Tolerance and pluralism had been
widely practiced, and even endorsed by the state. Foreigners exiled to the city had been free to worship as they
pleased. Yet in one moment all the open-mindedness of
Babylon dissolved into a fiercely intolerant mandate. The
antichrist spirit had seized the mind of Nebuchadnezzar,
driving his command that the greatest men of Babylon
worship the image or face execution.

Three young Jewish men stood still while the crowd surrounding them bowed in one submissive wave. All those
years that they had resisted the harlot's pleasures in their private lives made resisting Nebuchadnezzar's command second nature. They didn't even flinch at the thought of drawing
back in the face of death. Whether they lived or died was
inconsequential to them. One thing was certain: they would
not join Nebuchadnezzar's rebellion against God.

The king of Babylon watched them, disbelieving, his
face slowly distorting with indignation. The moment of
shock and silence ended abruptly. Venom and fury spewed
forth as Nebuchadnezzar ordered immediate death. Almost
before he finished speaking, the three were seized by the
royal guard. The king was outraged, and all the leaders of
Babylonia would witness the fate of those who would not
worship the image.[3] The young Jews stood strong, though
it meant certain death.

Executioners led them in bonds to a furnace whose
fire was so ravenous it incinerated the very servants who

---

[3]   This is a foreshadowing of Revelation 13:15.

were to throw them in. But the fire that was designed to demonstrate the king's wrath would instead be the fire Yahweh had ordained to manifest His glory. God's fiery love and zeal for His own made that furnace seem cool in comparison. To the shock of all, the fires that were meant to demonstrate the wrath of Babylon were instead demonstrating the supernatural might of the Jewish God. In pure amazement, Nebuchadnezzar peered into the furnace and saw the Lord standing with His people in the midst of the fire. Recognizing the irresistible sovereignty of their God, Nebuchadnezzar quickly ordered the furnace to be opened. When the Jewish people were brought forth unscorched from the fires of Babylon, their faith in God had not only been tested and purified, but publicly vindicated. Faced with death, Daniel's three friends considered the glory of God to be of greater value than their own lives.

The Pride of Babylon

Nebuchadnezzar's awe of the Most High would not last long. On one beautiful evening, he was walking atop the roof of his palace, surveying the legendary beauty of terraced stonework and lush hanging gardens. Oh, the view of the city from there! He looked around at the city he had built. The setting sun glimmered off the towers and temples that littered Babylon's horizon. He could still remember planning the layout of the city. He thought of the valiant military campaigns he had executed to finance it. He remembered drawing the plans to finish the Tower of Babel. Now it was all before him. All his plans had been accomplished and everything he had dreamed had been realized. Pride began to swell in his heart. In the glory of that moment, Nebuchadnezzar uttered a blasphemy that would expel him from human society:

> Is not this great Babylon, which I have built with
> my mighty power as a royal residence and for
> the glory of my majesty?
>
> —Daniel 4:30

Satan had been driven from heaven because he desired to make himself like the Most High. Adam and Eve had been driven from the garden by the desire to become as God, knowing good and evil. The Babelites were dispersed because they wanted to make a name for themselves. Now the king of Babylon had succumbed to the same fate. The desire for human glory intoxicated Nebuchadnezzar; he was drunk with the wine of the harlot.

With the words of his blasphemy still in his mouth, God released His judgment upon the king:

> Seven periods of time shall pass over you, until
> you know that the Most High rules the kingdom
> of men and gives it to whom He will.
>
> —Daniel 4:32

God's judgment came like a lightning strike out of blue sky. For years, the most powerful man on earth lived among animals and ate grass like an ox. One moment Nebuchadnezzar was basking in the glory of the most powerful position in the world; the next moment he had lost it all.

The Empire Falls

The suddenness of God's judgment on Nebuchadnezzar was a foreshadowing of how swiftly the Babylonian Empire would fall only a few decades later. The end of the Babylonian Empire would come during the reign of Nebuchadnezzar's grandson, Belshazzar. The night of Babylon's fall would begin with a royal feast celebrating the pomp of the empire and end with the invasion of a foreign power.[4] Like the confusion of tongues that came in a moment to the Babelites thousands of years before, the Babylonian empire came to an end with shocking abruptness.

Only a few short decades after Nebuchadnezzar's death, the empire began to falter. The Persian army was now on the march and there was little the poorly-led Babylonian army could do about it. The Persian army routed the Babylonians just outside their own capital city. Accepting defeat, the Babylonian army retreated within the safety of the city walls. Once inside, they were sure there was nothing more the Persians could do. These were the impenetrable walls that Nebuchadnezzar had constructed. The double walls of the city extended for miles. They were twenty-five feet thick and over forty feet high. There was no way for the Persians to get through them. The city of Babylon was impregnably enclosed.

When the news reached King Belshazzar that Cyrus had ordered a siege of Babylon, he scoffed. Confident that his city was too well equipped and protected for the Persian siege to be successful, Belshazzar ordered a royal celebration. No expense was spared; every treasure of Babylon was on full display. The very vessels that had been looted from the temple in Jerusalem were used as wine goblets for Belshazzar and his concubines (Dan. 5:3).

While the royal feast raged on inside the walls of Babylon, the Persian army made a surprising move. Rather than positioning themselves for a siege, they moved upstream on the Euphrates River, away from Babylon. They didn't make a single embankment. They made no attempt to get over the mighty walls. Instead they began to construct some sort

[4] Dan. 5.

of dam. The entire army worked tirelessly, moving the dirt from the banks of the river into its stream so that the course of the river was diverted into a soggy marsh. The flow of the mighty river into Babylon began to slow. Once the water level of the river was low enough, the Persian army waded under the city's wall and entered Babylon. With no way to get over the wall, they had gone under it.[5]

When the Persians entered the city, King Cyrus was welcomed as a hero and liberator of Babylon. The citizens of Babylon had come to so detest their leaders that they were ready for a new king. All those who had been taken into captivity recognized Cyrus as their ticket home. With a single command, Cyrus executed Belshazzar and assumed control of Babylon. In one night, the mighty Babylonian Empire vanished from history.

The End of Captivity

As the new king of Babylon, Cyrus ordered freedom for all who had been taken captive, even promising to finance the return of the Jewish people to Jerusalem. God's purpose for His people in Babylon had ended and the years of exile were completed.

> In the first year of Cyrus king of Persia, that the word of the LORD by the mouth of Jeremiah might be fulfilled, the LORD stirred up the spirit of Cyrus king of Persia, so that he made a proclamation throughout all his kingdom and also put it in writing: "Thus says Cyrus king of Persia: The LORD, the God of heaven, has given me all the kingdoms of the earth, and he has charged me to build him a house at Jerusalem, which is

[5]   Miller, *NAC: Daniel*, 166f.

in Judah. Whoever is among you of all his people, may his God be with him, and let him go up
to Jerusalem . . . and rebuild the house of the
LORD."

—Ezra 1:1–3

The captivity was over. The spiritual season of discipline and training through the pressures of Babylon had
come to an end. God now called His people to come out
of Babylon to rebuild the temple in Jerusalem!

While Cyrus' declaration was nothing short of a miracle, the glorious news was met with indifference by many
of the Jews living in Babylon. Now that it was possible to
return to the land of Judah, many actually preferred to stay
in Babylon. Over the past decades, their roots had grown
deep into the great city. Their families, community, and
businesses were well established. Their reasons seemed
innocuous, and they were still attending the synagogues,
but they had in reality fallen prey to compromise with the
harlot; choosing temporal comfort, they had forsaken the
infinitely greater pleasure of fulfilling God's purpose in their
generation.[6] They had traded the call of God on their lives
for the temporary luxury and prosperity of Babylon.

There was, however, a remnant who had not fallen to
Babylon's power, who, like Daniel, had grown in love for God.
Many had continued in prayer and fasting, living without
compromise and proclaiming God's supremacy even while
in captivity. Divine destiny awaited those who responded to
God's call to come out of Babylon's confusion and return to

[6] Jews who did not return to Jerusalem after the captivity continued to
call Babylon their home until they became an unwanted population.
Ultimately they were expelled from the city of Babylon to Seleucia,
where they suffered a great slaughter at the hands of Greeks and
Arabs. See Josephus, *The Complete Works*, 601.

Jerusalem. God was not just calling them back to a place; He was calling them to their destiny as His people.

The captivity had a purifying effect of sifting out the insincere, as well as strengthening the resolve of the faithful. Jerusalem would never again return to the idolatry that had plagued it before the captivity. Those who survived the fires of Babylon were set like flint on fulfilling God's plan for the city of Jerusalem.

E I G H T

THE RESTORATION

GOD WAS AGAIN TURNING HIS FACE towards Jerusalem. His dwelling place had been desolate for nearly fifty years, but the desire to dwell with His people never stopped burning. After the captivity one thing was clear: He would not dwell with a half-hearted people. God would rather His house were torn down by pagans and His people exiled than tolerate lukewarm affections for His glory. But now that the captivity was over, God was stirring the spirit of a new generation for the house of the Lord.

In the days before the exile, Jeremiah had relentlessly called the nation to repentance, but his call had been met with cold apathy; now the Jewish people were eager to obey. Sin had once blinded the nation of Judah and deluded its leadership; now their leaders were zealous to serve the purpose of God for their generation. Before Babylon there was no one to stand in the gap before God on behalf of the nation; now an entire priesthood was longing for the day when true intercession would again take place in Jerusalem. Had it really worked? Had the captivity successfully trained a generation of wholehearted worshipers of God?

Or would the excitement over Jerusalem wane and leave the nation in spiritual apathy? Only time would tell.

The Foundation

When Cyrus decreed freedom for the Jewish people to return to Jerusalem, a new generation packed up and began the long journey home. They were the Lord's new army. Most of them had never seen Jerusalem before. On the long journey home they talked incessantly of the past glory of Jerusalem—glory that they had only heard about in bedtime stories. The Lord had so filled them with dreams for the future of Jerusalem that they couldn't help but spill over with giddiness concerning the calling of their generation. With excited gestures and laughter, they planned the restoration of their nation. Zerubbabel, son of Shealtiel and rightful heir to David's throne, led the joyful company through the hills of Judah until they could see their beloved city in the distance. They quickened their pace as they neared Jerusalem.

The joyful demeanor of the group quickly dissipated as they arrived upon a shocking scene of devastation. Solomon's temple, once the glory of Israel, had been razed to the foundations, its splendor reduced to a heap of ashes. The entire city had been laid waste by the Babylonian army. Decades of neglect had only increased the original destruction. Rebuilding the house of the Lord was going to be an enormous project; the new arrivals felt completely overwhelmed.

With nothing else to do, they began the slow work of rebuilding the temple. But before laying a single brick, they attended to the most needful thing. One priority preceded all others: to reestablish the altar and the daily sacrifices

(Ezra 3:2–3). From the very beginning, the high priest—Joshua, the son of Jozadak—determined that night and day prayer would be the context in which the rest of the work would be done. Intercession was the cornerstone of the temple.

With the hearts of the people united in partnership to God through prayer, the reconstruction was taking shape more rapidly than anyone had imagined. Zerubbabel was working closely with Joshua. Side by side, the heir to the throne of Jerusalem and the high priest led their generation into God's purpose. The foundation of the temple was being established. The days were long and the labor was backbreaking, but divine momentum carried them through each day. Every brick they set was one brick closer to their dream. Through years of wholehearted worship and faithful labor, the foundations of the temple were laid.

The Opposition

The news of the Jewish temple began to spread through the region. And it soon became apparent that Satan would not let the Jewish restoration go unopposed. He understood what was at stake and would stop at nothing to thwart God's plan to reestablish His Bethel in the earth. Soon the neighboring nations of Judah began to approach Zerubbabel in hopes that he would abandon his exclusive religious aims in favor of linking arms with the wider regional community. They came to him, promising assistance in rebuilding the temple so that they might all share it:

> Let us build with you, for we worship your God as you do, and we have been sacrificing to Him.
>
> —Ezra 4:2

This was an intriguing offer. Much could be gained if Judah created an allegiance with their neighbors. Not only would they enjoy greater security, but the Jews would be assisted in rebuilding the temple. They could certainly have used the extra labor and resources. By compromising his nation and joining his neighbors, Zerubbabel could expedite the building project and strengthen his political relationships in the region.

But the cloak of religious universalism wouldn't work on Zerubbabel. He had been forged in the fires of Babylon. The other nations may very well have offered sacrifices to the God of the Hebrews, but their sacrifices were offered to other gods as well. Zerubbabel had lived his entire life resisting the poisonous wine of Babylon's religious pluralism and he wasn't about to yield now that the welfare of his fledgling nation was at stake (Ezra 4:3). Zerubbabel forcefully declined the invitation as nothing less than an attempt to subvert the restoration of Jerusalem.

But Zerubbabel's refusal to compromise with the pagans was not taken lightly. Satan stirred up the enemies of the Jewish people to harass them even further, frustrating their every effort to rebuild. King Cyrus, who had been so favorable to the Jewish people, was killed in battle, and there was a new king on the throne—one whose political interests in the region were shaped by the voices outside of Judah. Once it became apparent that the Jews were fully intent on rebuilding Jerusalem without political compromise, the enemies of Jerusalem knew there was only one way to stop them. They pressured the king of Persia to see things their way. King Artaxerxes commanded that the rebuilding of the temple cease.

When the king's decree was read to the Jewish leaders,

they were crushed. It was over. God's purpose in calling them out of Babylon had been defeated. Their enemies had succeeded; they could do nothing to alter or resist Artaxerxes' order. The Jewish people were militarily defenseless and politically anemic. Seeing no alternative, they complied with the royal decree and halted all their efforts to rebuild the house of the Lord.

Shrinking Back

With the rebuilding of the temple now strictly prohibited, Judah's national attention turned to restoring the life of its people. They put all of their efforts into reestablishing their own homes. The people began to work the ground, which had become arid and weedy over decades of neglect. Year in and year out they labored to establish their lives on the land.

Not surprisingly, their enemies, who had for so long harassed every attempt to rebuild the temple, shrugged with disinterest at the Jewish reprioritization. Satan couldn't care less that the people of God were modifying their homes, as long as it was at the expense of their purpose in God. The kingdom of hell was only threatened by the Jewish nation working in partnership with the God of heaven.

The Israelites had become accustomed to a certain standard of living while in Babylon, and their taste for it was not gone now that they were in their own land. They became preoccupied with making their own lives as comfortable as possible. The residual negative influences of the Babylonian captivity began to haunt them. The pressures that the Jewish people endured while in exile had followed them home, enticing them to compromise even in the promised land.

God's Discipline

But in spite of their self-centered labor, the land was not producing what they needed; they found themselves in a strange predicament. The more they strove for great agricultural harvests, the more their crops failed. The more they tried to turn profits in business, the more they found themselves in lack at the end of the day. The more time they spent establishing their life in the land, the more time it took to establish anything. Year after year, droughts plagued the land.[1] Food shortages and poverty were overtaking the people. Serious frustrations set in as some began to question why they had left the prosperity of Babylon for a life of futility in Judah.

Dissatisfaction lingered in the air over Jerusalem. The captivity was over, yet the Jews were still held captive to the will of their enemies. They were supposed to be rebuilding the temple, but the decree of King Artaxerxes had brought that to an end. They had turned to rebuilding their lives in the land, but all of their efforts to reestablish life in Jerusalem were failing. Droughts ravaged the land. The economy of Judah refused to grow. It wasn't supposed to be like this. Where was the God who had called them out of Babylon to Jerusalem and promised the restoration of the temple?

The people of God were caught in a spiritual maelstrom. They couldn't see it, but they had become a battlefield. Unseen forces were at work and everything hinged on the temple in Jerusalem. The Jewish people would have to decide between two options: continue to rebuild the temple at the risk of facing the wrath of their enemies, or abandon the temple altogether and risk something far

---

[1]   Baldwin, *TOTC: Haggai, Zechariah, Malachi*, 27.

worse. Satan wasn't the only one involved in this battle. High above the realm of men and demons, the sovereign God had commanded the rebuilding of His house in Jerusalem, and neither the decree of Artaxerxes nor Satan's activity had the power to overturn it.

Haggai and Zechariah

Finally God broke the silence and awakened the prophetic voices in Judah. He sent forth His Word to accomplish His decree for Jerusalem. To give voice to His heart, God set in place the forerunners of the day. These faithful prophets maintained a heavenly perspective in spite of the confusion that had overtaken the nation. By the Spirit of God, they understood what was at stake. The prophet Haggai and his younger contemporary Zechariah began to call the children of Israel back into the purpose of God. The word of the Lord burned in Haggai as he lifted his voice:

> Thus says the LORD of hosts: "These people say the time has not yet come to rebuild the house of the LORD . . . Is it a time for you yourselves to dwell in your paneled houses, while this house lies in ruins? Now, therefore, thus says the Lord of hosts: Consider your ways. You have sown much, and harvested little. You eat, but you never have enough; you drink, but you never have your fill. You clothe yourselves, but no one is warm. And he who earns wages does so to put them into a bag with holes." Thus says the LORD of hosts: "Consider your ways. Go up to the hills and bring wood and build the house, that I may take pleasure in it and that I may be glorified," says the LORD. "You looked

for much, and behold it came to little. And when
you brought it home, I blew it away. Why?" declares the Lord of hosts. "Because of my house
that lies in ruins, while each of you busies himself with his own house."

—Haggai 1:2–9

God's message to His people was clear; their best efforts and resources were being spent on the wrong thing.
Their vision had become so myopic and focused on their
own lives that they had lost all sight of God and His glory.
They had forsaken their God-given calling for the temporal
pleasures of "living well." They were a chosen generation
choosing something less than what they were made for.
But the Lord would not allow it. He was blowing away the
temporal-mindedness of His people by frustrating their
carnal living. In His great mercy, God was purposely ruin-
ing their livelihood so that they might choose to take hold
of the eternal.

Joshua's Invitation

The word of the Lord—carried by the prophets Haggai
and Zechariah—was not primarily directed to the people of
Judah; it was first and foremost a message for Judah's leaders. The people had fallen victim to the influences of living
in Babylon, and God was calling Joshua and Zerubbabel to
lead the nation out of her perilous spiritual condition.

The prophet Zechariah was given a vision exposing
the hidden war against Jerusalem's destiny. In the prophetic vision, Zechariah saw Satan standing in the heavenly courtroom. Satan was standing before the Judge of
the universe as the great prosecutor, leveling accusation
after accusation against Joshua. He aimed to spiritually

neutralize Jerusalem's primary intercessor. With venomous passion, he argued that Joshua had been disqualified as Jerusalem's high priest due to sin. Joshua had no ground to defend himself. Clothed in filthy rags, he knew he was guilty of every accusation.

Joshua had no hope of acquittal until the Judge made a shocking move. In a display of sovereign grace and burning zeal for Jerusalem, the Judge stepped down from His bench and became Joshua's advocate. With one judicial decision, the Judge of the universe rebuked Satan and pardoned Joshua of every charge. Joshua's filthy rags were exchanged for spotless garments of white. Then the Lord turned and spoke to Joshua: "If you walk in my way and keep my charge, then you shall rule my house and have charge of my courts, and I will give you the right of access among those who are standing here" (Zech. 3:7).

The Lord extended a conditional invitation to Joshua. If Joshua set his heart to walk in the way of the Lord, he would have total access to the heavenly court. It was a direct invitation into the governmental epicenter of the universe, the place where eternal decrees were given, where God's strategies were implemented. Archangels stood at the ready and demons trembled for the decisions made in that courtroom. The greatest kings of the earth were subject to the consequence of every verdict made there. And Joshua was offered an all-access pass.

Every critical event in Jerusalem had its inception in the spiritual realm. From the order of King Cyrus to rebuild the temple to the decree of Artaxerxes to halt it, supernatural forces prevailed upon the hearts of men. Because of the central role of Jerusalem in God's eternal plans, angels and demons were at war over its destiny.[2]

The nation of Judah would not experience the full blessing that God had in His heart unless they asked for it. God refused to impose the grace of heaven on unwilling subjects. Before God released His ordained blessing for Judah, Joshua would have to enter the court of heaven as Judah's spiritual leader; he would have to travail in prayer, in partnership with God's heart and power, to call it forth. Through the ministry of intercession, Joshua was invited to become a human conduit to bring forth God's will on earth as it was in heaven. Intercession was the only way Jerusalem would see her temple restored.

The Stranger in Babylon

Prayer would pave the way, but prayer would not rebuild the temple. No matter how much prayer was offered, Joshua would never wake up some morning to find that God had built the temple Himself. God wasn't going to finish the temple using His angels; He was going to do it in partnership with His people.

As a nation, Judah needed to obey its calling. The people needed to repent of the temporal pursuits that had bogged them down in spiritual confusion and live in the light of eternity. To do this, the people needed leadership, a leader whose lifestyle and example carried more authority than his official title. It couldn't just be another king in name only; the man had to have a royal heart.

Zerubbabel was the rightful heir to David's throne. But because of the political pressures of the Persian Empire, the nation dared not officially proclaim him king. Such a treacherous declaration would be quickly and severely

---

[2] This is a war with a predetermined outcome, but a war nonetheless.

punished. Though he would never publicly be declared king, Zerubbabel had proven himself to be one over the years. He had led the Jewish people back to Jerusalem and rejected the compromising offers of Judah's enemies. He had faithfully served the interests of the nation and deeply desired the purpose of God for his generation. Even though Judah could not publicly crown Zerubbabel, they still looked to him as their king.

Before Jerusalem, Zerubbabel had been born and raised as a captive in Babylon, though he had always been strangely out of place there. It hadn't mattered that many of his Jewish neighbors and family found life in Babylon quite pleasant. Zerubbabel longed for the city of Jerusalem. From his youth he had dreamt of the day when he would return and reestablish God's house. His friends had never understood and would often ask why he was so deeply moved to return to the desolate city of Jerusalem when things were so prosperous in Babylon.

Zerubbabel's name reflected his destiny.[3] His name meant "stranger in Babylon." Unlike many others who had let Babylon capture their affections, Zerubbabel kept his heart for the Lord. He certainly wasn't perfect, but he refused to fall in love with the Babylonian way. He would not settle for anything less than God's promise for Jerusalem. Even on the days when it seemed that he would not live to see Jerusalem, he held firm. He was deeply in love with God and His Jerusalem, and remained a stranger in Babylon until the day he left captivity.[4]

[3] The last part of his name is obviously "Babel," which means Babylon. "Zerub" is translated as "seed" or "descendant," meaning quite simply that he was born in Babylon. The first part of Zerubbabel's name can be derived from the word "zuwr" meaning "foreign" or "strange." Hitchcock, "Zerubbabel," *Hitchcock's Bible Names Dictionary*.

[4] Zerubbabel wasn't alone in his longing for the city of God. Though

Zerubbabel could never be publicly proclaimed as Judah's king, yet he was ordained to rise in the time of national crisis to become, in every respect, a king. Royalty was in his blood and in his soul, a true descendant of David. The pressures of Babylon had shaped Zerubbabel's character, and his noble heart was inflamed by God's zeal for Jerusalem.

The Valley of Decision

Zerubbabel had never faced anything like this. His life had been filled with many trials and temptations but not on the scale of what now stood before him. Haggai and Zechariah would not relent; God's message was clear. The time had come to rebuild the house of prayer. But enormous obstacles stood in the way. King Artaxerxes' decree had never been rescinded; it was still in effect. If Zerubbabel obeyed the message of God, it could cost him his life.

Zerubbabel understood what it meant to disobey the decree of a Persian king and wasn't making this decision lightly. While Zerubbabel he pondered this, the prophet Zechariah brought a message from the Lord regarding the temple.

> This is the word of the Lord to Zerubbabel: "Not by might, nor by power, but by my Spirit," says the LORD of hosts. "Who are you, O great mountain? Before Zerubbabel you shall become a plain. And he shall bring forward the top stone amid shouts of 'Grace, grace to it!'"
>
> —Zechariah 4:6–7

the citizens of Babylon often compelled the Jewish people to entertain them with native songs, those whose hearts were out of place in Babylon and longed for Jerusalem took up a lament instead: "By the waters of Babylon, there we sat down and wept, when we remembered Zion . . . For there our captors required of us songs . . . How shall we sing the LORD's song in a foreign land?" (Ps. 137:1–4).

Zerubbabel had nothing to worry about. The restoration of the house of the Lord would not be accomplished by human power; it would be brought into being entirely by divine grace. Judah's national weakness was inconsequential. No power of man or devil could withstand a movement of this magnitude. The very power that had created the universe was empowering Zerubbabel. The temple was still half-finished, but the Spirit of God had already secured its outcome; it would be finished by the irresistible power of the grace of God.

The heavenly decree had been given; the victory already won. Now all that remained was for it to be realized. Through the courageous leadership of Zerubbabel and the intercession of Joshua, the Israelites began to rebuild the temple. As the people of God began to respond according to His purposes in Jerusalem, the past vanities of Babylon lost its power over them. The aimlessness and spiritual confusion vanished as they embraced the God-ordained purpose for their generation.

The Commanded Blessing

As expected, Judah's enemies took note of their activity. Attempting to intimidate the Jewish people into compliance, they came asking who was responsible for this latest act of treason. They took a list of names of all who dared defy the empire. They sent their report to the king of Persia, expecting a decisive response.

But there was a new king on the throne, by the name of Darius. Unlike Artaxerxes, the new king wasn't poisoned against the Jews. He wanted to find out for himself the story of the much-maligned Jews. The king demanded that the royal archives be searched to find what past kings had written, and the original decree of Cyrus was found. As Darius read the Persian decree to free the Jews from Babylon, he knew what he had to do. King Darius was stirred by God's sovereign power and gave the royal decree:

> I make a decree regarding what you shall do for these elders of the Jews for the rebuilding of this house of God. The cost is to be paid to these men in full and without delay from the royal revenue . . . And whatever is needed . . . let that be given to them day by day without fail.
>
> —Ezra 6:8–9

To the dismay of Judah's enemies, their appeal to the king had completely backfired. Rather than halting the restoration, it financed its completion. God had emptied their every threat. Just as He promised, the Spirit of God demolished every obstacle that stood before Zerubbabel. The danger that once seemed insurmountable turned out to be a mirage, nothing more than a paper tiger. The mountains that once skewed Zerubbabel's vision were gone. The Lord had cut down everything that opposed His purposes for Jerusalem.

When the people of Judah turned away from the self-serving values of Babylon, they experienced God's overflowing provision. Rain fell on the land once again; their crops abounded. Unimaginable wealth poured in to support the rebuilding. The riches of the world that had once been brought to Babylon began to be distributed to God's kingdom. In one divine moment, every imaginable resource came to the aid of the Jewish people. They went from self-seeking lack to God-seeking superabundance as they gave their hearts to rebuilding the house of prayer in

Jerusalem. The Lord had raised up one pagan king, Cyrus, to finance the beginning of His work. Now He raised up another, Darius, to finance its completion.

Four great souls refined in the fires of Babylon led the Jewish people back to rebuilding the temple. The forerunners Haggai and Zechariah declared the prophetic heart of God and encouraged the leaders of Judah. The intercession of Joshua released the government of heaven into the earth. And Zerubbabel, a "stranger in Babylon," was divinely empowered to lead his generation to fulfill the purpose of God.

The temple was finished and dedicated in 516 BC. Seventy years had elapsed between the final exile in 586 BC and the restoration of the temple. In those years God took a rebellious and idolatrous nation and made them an army of wholehearted worshipers. The years of captivity in Babylon had deeply shaped a new generation. The fires of Babylon had refined the hearts of God's people. Though the journey was long and difficult, the Lord brought His people through the captivity into restoration. The temple was finished; the Lord's presence returned. The gateway of heaven was once again opened in the earth through God's house of prayer in Jerusalem.

Jerusalem's Once and Future Prophecy

Babylon would never be the same after the Persian Empire. The harlot queen had fallen from her throne. The great city that once enjoyed unequalled power became just another city in the vast Persian Empire. Babylon continued to be one of the greatest cities in the earth, but it would never return to the power it possessed under Nebuchadnezzar.

In the fires of Babylonian exile, the people of God were forced to focus their affections on God. The captivity was a training ground. They had to spiritually discern and consistently resist the seduction of Babylon. Those who did not, lost their way and revealed their true citizenship. But those who persevered were transformed into authentic lovers of God. Refined in Babylon, an entire generation was used by God to rebuild the house of prayer in Jerusalem.

> Jeremiah wrote in a book all the disaster that should come upon Babylon, all these words that are written concerning Babylon. And Jeremiah said to Seraiah: "When you come to Babylon, see that you read all these words, and say, 'O Lord, you have said concerning this place that you will cut it off, so that nothing shall dwell in it, neither man nor beast, and it shall be desolate forever.' When you finish reading this book, tie a stone to it and cast it into the midst of the Euphrates, and say, 'Thus shall Babylon sink, to rise no more, because of the disaster that I am bringing upon her, and they shall become exhausted." Thus far are the words of Jeremiah.
>
> —Jeremiah 51:60–64

The Lord cut off the power of the Babylonian Empire in a moment, but the total destruction of Babylon promised by God was not fulfilled in the takeover by Cyrus' army. Unlike the devastation that befell Jerusalem in 586 BC, Babylon was conquered almost entirely bloodlessly.[5] Jeremiah's prophecy that Babylon would "sink, to rise no more" did not come to pass with the fall of the empire. The Babylonian

---

[5]   Of course King Belshazzar and a number of his officials were killed to officially end his reign.

Empire fell to Persia swiftly, but the utter destruction spoken of by Jeremiah would not come to pass until long after Babylon was abandoned hundreds of years later.[6]

Jeremiah foresaw the fall of the Babylonian Empire from the world stage in 539 BC, but he also saw something more. He was seeing in part what the apostle John saw fully on the isle of Patmos. By the Holy Spirit, John and Jeremiah saw both the judgment of the temporal manifestation of Babylon in their day and, more importantly, the ultimate demise of Babylon the Great at the close of this age, when Babylon will truly fall and never arise again.

Babylon continued long after the Babylonian Empire fell. The city lost its prominence, but over the years the spirit of Babylon only grew stronger. The harlot principality would find another city to call home, far west of the land of Shinar and long after the Babylonian Empire had vanished. The great harlot returned in the first century AD in its most sinister and powerful expression yet: Rome.

---

[6] See Part III.

PART III

THE ROMAN EMPIRE

NINE
THE NEW BABYLON

IT WAS HAPPENING AGAIN. Nearly three hundred years after Nebuchadnezzar, Babylon was positioned to re-emerge as the world's capital. The greatest conquest in history was unfolding and its path led to the famed gates of the great city. Like a seductive harlot beckoning a prospective client, Babylon was luring a new king with the promise of untold glory.

The king of Macedon had taken the world by storm in less than a decade. His unrelenting march began in Greece and spread like wildfire through the entire Mediterranean. At twenty-three years of age, he was crowned Pharaoh of Egypt, and by the age of twenty-six, he overcame and controlled the vast Persian Empire. The world had witnessed many conquerors, but never one like this. This was Alexander.

The gates of Babylon swung open to welcome her new king. Alexander led a triumphant procession through the Ishtar Gate. In a ceremony eerily reminiscent of ancient coronations, Alexander was crowned king of Babylon. With grand visions to rebuild the ancient city to new heights of glory, Alexander determined to make it the capital of the greatest empire in history.[1] Once again Babylon was poised to dominate the world, this time through the throne of Alexander the Great.

The city of Babylon was ready to reclaim her throne. But Babylon's time would have to wait. A shocking event would turn the tide of history and rob the harlot city of the furthering of her legacy.[2] Alexander would not live long enough to see the city of Babylon established as his new power base. The greatest conqueror in history mysteriously died within the city at the age of thirty-three.

A Divided Empire

In the aftermath of his sudden death, Alexander's vast empire was divided between his generals. The lines were drawn and territories appropriated. The Babylonian region of the shattered empire fell to General Seleucus. The region, which included Babylon and Jerusalem, would be ruled by the Seleucids for the next 250 years.

The death of Alexander the Great had effectively sealed the fate of Babylon. Unlike Alexander, King Seleucus had no interest in restoring the ancient city. Serious decay over the long ages of her illustrious history was taking its toll. And to compound the problem, the Euphrates River had changed course so that it no longer ran along the city. Privileged Babylon had lost her geographic advantage and Seleucus decided that ancient Babylon should be deserted in favor of a new location. Hoping in vain that

---

[1]   Though Persia had a number of cities of major political importance and Susa as its capital (Dan. 8:2; Esth. 1:2; Neh. 1:1), Babylon was Alexander's choice.

[2]   With Alexander's dynamic leadership, the ancient city would almost certainly have arisen to new heights.

the glory of Babylon could be recreated, he ordered that a new Babylon be constructed nearly forty miles north of the ancient city. The task was enormous. It was nothing less than an attempt to transplant the greatest city in the world. Some of the intact building materials from the old site were transported to the new city. When New Babylon was finished, it was only a shell of what Nebuchadnezzar had accomplished. Seleucus ordered the old city to be abandoned and New Babylon to be populated.[3] As the final caravans left the city, the glory of ancient Babylon faded from history.

Hellenism

The culture and language of Greece swept the world in the wake of Alexander's conquest. The world was united like never before. Every territory he conquered had been assimilated. From Europe to Asia, the earth shared a common language. Not since the initial days of the Tower of Babel had language so connected the people on earth. But the effects of Hellenism went beyond the Greek language. Alexander's policy to absorb and adopt the pagan ideas of conquered cultures united the world in religion, commerce, and culture. After Alexander, the world was a smaller place.

Nowhere else were the effects of Hellenism being felt more severely than in the little nation of Israel. God's people were battling to retain their distinctive identity in the face of a tidal wave of paganism. They were fighting to stay faithful. Their traditions were under fire. The pervasive influence of Greece that had swept the world was threatening to sweep God's nation along with it. Under the

[3] This city was also known as Seleucia-on-the-Tigris. Today this city is called Baghdad.

political power of the Seleucids, the pressure to compromise was fierce. When the Jewish people firmly refused to let go of their ancient traditions, their resistance to Hellenism was met by military force.

On the eve of 166 BC, the nation of Israel faced an antichrist power that would permanently mark the psyche of the Jewish people. The leader of the Seleucid region, Antiochus IV (Epiphanes), marched into Israel in a campaign to annihilate the Jewish faith. He commanded that the Jews dissolve their religious laws and ordered the brutal deaths of those who continued to circumcise their sons.[4] But it wasn't the murder of innocents that forever fixed Antiochus Epiphanes as the prototypical Antichrist figure in Jewish history. It was the "abomination of desolation." In an act that was meant to break the resilience of the Jewish people, Antiochus set up an altar to the Greek god Zeus in Zerubbabel's temple. The ritual act of demon worship desecrated the innermost sanctuary, an abomination that utterly defiled the temple in Jerusalem. God's house of prayer, the place where His glory and presence dwelt, was desolated.

The brutal oppression of Antiochus Epiphanes outraged the Jewish people. With no other alternative, a brave few took up arms. The courageous military leadership of a ragtag army inspired the nation. They determined to drive the pagan oppressors out of Judea. The first of the offensives were successful, but over the years of turmoil the little nation of Israel needed to create other national alliances to stave off the constant pressure that the Seleucid kings applied. The leadership in Israel felt it had to turn to the latest world power for help. So the high priests in Jerusalem sent emissaries to Rome.

[4] Josephus, *The Complete Works*, 388.

The New Babylon

A new star was rising on the world scene. What had begun as an eccentric little settlement had quickly burgeoned into a global empire. Established on the bank of the Tiber River, the city of Rome had been developing for centuries, attracting men from all over the Mediterranean. Starting as a melting pot of people and ideas, the city of Rome soon grew into a regional power that successfully unified the Roman peninsula. The unequalled skill of Rome's professional army meant she quickly conquered her neighbors and dominated the eastern Mediterranean. The army systematically slaughtered and enslaved all who resisted them.

By the first century, the Romans were the greatest political power in the world. The ancient city of Babylon had long faded from significance. Rome was the new center of world culture and trade. The city of Babylon had once given rise to the latest advances in architecture and the arts. Now Rome was surpassing the ancient city in every respect. Rome was taking up where ancient Babylon had left off.[5]

This was more than just a city. Behind Rome's magnificent marble temples, colonnades, and enormous coliseums was a dark ideology. Its people believed Rome had been chosen by the gods to rule the world and lead a united humanity into a golden age. Romantic notions of a nearing utopian era hung in the air. Every military victory and every conquered city was further proof of Rome's unfolding destiny. The empire was built on the dream of uniting

---

[5] Saint Augustine, the great theologian and leader of the Church in the fifth century AD, understood that Rome had become the new Babylon. In his famous work *The City of God*, Augustine writes, "To be brief, the city of Rome was founded, like another Babylon, and as it were the daughter of the former Babylon . . . Rome was founded, as it were another Babylon in the west." Augustine, *The City of God*, 749.

the world through religion and commerce—a civilization that would realize the full potential of human achievement. Rome wasn't just a city; it was a vision for humanity: a vision called "eternal Rome."

But Rome wasn't merely a dark utopian ideology either. Above all else, the empire of Rome was a religion. Possessing a comprehensive system of beliefs and values, the message of the imperial cult was as religious as it was political.[6] No distinction was made between religion and state. Spirituality, commerce, and politics were viewed as part of one imperial reality. A dark network of demonic beliefs and idolatrous practices entangled the world as the cities of the empire became a worldwide religious web. This evil system of false religion was integrated with both the commercial and cultural enterprises of Rome.

A true Roman citizen also needed to embrace religious pluralism as a way of life. Gods of the earth, gods of the heaven, and gods of the sea were equally worshiped.[7] Those who did not embrace the pantheon were considered despicable atheists.[8] Loyalty to Rome was the greatest virtue a Roman could possess. Wealth, power, and honor were guaranteed to those who demonstrated the highest levels of devotion and loyalty. On the other hand, disloyalty to Rome was rewarded with crucifixion. No fate was deemed too cruel for an enemy of the empire.

But the centerpiece of the religion of Rome was her lord and savior: Caesar. Images of him could be found

[6] For a fascinating study of religion and power in Roman imperial society, see Horsley, *Paul and Empire*, 1997.

[7] As long as a religious practice was not perceived as a threat to the stability of the empire, it was endorsed by the state or at least tolerated by regional governors. Many mystery religions were outlawed because of the threat they posed to Roman order.

[8] This is why Jews and Christians were often labeled "atheists" in Rome.

in every city and temple of the empire. Sanctuaries were dedicated to him. The currency bore his image. Caesar imposed upon every facet of life. He was the provider and protector of Rome; he had brought peace and justice to the world. Every Roman looked to Caesar as his personal benefactor. Allegiance and loyalty were Caesar's imperial due. As the executive power and patron of the new Babylon, Caesar stood as one of the gods; he was the latest embodiment of the king of Babylon.

As time wore on, the Roman Empire became drunk with sexual immorality. Illicit sexual practices spread through the empire as widespread perversion became progressively stronger and more twisted. Pagan temple prostitution, homosexuality, and public orgies became commonplace. No sexual practice was taboo. These perversions were exported from Rome to the rest of the world. The great city reached into every crevasse of the known world, filling it with her sensual lusts.

The greatest luxuries in the world were imported and exported from Rome. Merchants from around the world traveled to the great city to do business, growing rich from the city's luxurious and decadent lifestyle. From the trading of wares to the selling of human slaves like livestock, Rome was the center of global commerce. The city gorged on every kind of luxury and corrupted all those who could be bought and sold with her riches.

The demonic power that had inspired Nimrod and Nebuchadnezzar to build the gateway of the gods had seduced a new generation.[9] The vision of an "eternal Rome" baited

---

[9] New Testament exegete George Eldon Ladd writes, "Babylon had an embodiment in first-century Rome (1 Pet. 5:13); and in Jewish-Christian apocalyptic, Babylon became a symbolic name for Rome." Ladd, *Revelation of John,* 194.

the human race into another attempt to make a name for themselves (Gen. 11:4). Rome had become the great harlot. The kings of the earth wanted her favor. The merchants desired her riches. Rome had taken Babylon's place as the nerve center of a worldwide network of false religion and commerce. Drunk with the wine of her sexual immorality, the earth was succumbing to unprecedented depths of sin. Abortion, slavery, and oppression of the poor were all fully endorsed by the Roman ethic. Murderous entertainment was filling the coliseums for Romans whose lust for blood became insatiable. The gateway of the gods was opening through the Roman network of idolatrous religion. As Satan's dark kingdom was extended through human participation, demonic activity was reaching historic levels. Babylon was back. Once again the harlot had taken her throne. Her latest embodiment was first-century Rome.[10]

The New Captivity

A dark shadow had been cast over Israel. At first the Jewish people welcomed Roman assistance in their struggle against the Seleucids.[11] But asking benefits of Rome came with a price. In the chaotic days of Israel's fight for independence, the divisive struggle for power within the ranks of the Jewish leadership had effectively forfeited the nation's autonomy. With Rome's help, Israel defeated

---

[10] The Bible makes the connection between Rome and Babylon explicit. The apostle Peter makes specific reference to this in the closing of his first letter when he writes, "She who is at Babylon, who is likewise chosen, sends you greetings" (1 Pet. 5:13). Scholars agree almost unanimously that Peter is making a veiled reference to the city of Rome in this verse. It is highly unlikely that he is referring to the actual geographic city of Babylon, because it was already destroyed by the time Peter wrote his letter.

[11] The Roman senate offered to support the Jews against the Seleucids in 161 BC.

the Seleucids. But their victory had devastating consequences. From the moment the Romans were invited to
intervene in Israel's affairs until the Jews would be driven
from the promised land over a century later, they would be
subjects of Rome.[12]

Most of the Jewish people were deeply divided about
their situation. While a few like the tax collectors actually
enjoyed the benefits of Rome, most Jews hated the Romans, many because the empire protected the ruling class
of Israel. Others hated Rome out of religious zeal. They
could not tolerate the pagan influence pervading Judea.
Whether hatred for the empire rose from political or religious reasons, one thing was clear: subjection to Rome
had become the new captivity. The Jewish people were in
the promised land but not experiencing the promise. Rome
held sway over every dimension of the nation of Israel.

Many of the Jews did not take to their new subjugation
peacefully. Zealots spurred numerous rebellions to throw
off the Roman yoke. But the oppression of Rome had one
symbol that struck fear in even the bravest of insurrection-
ists: the Roman cross. An instrument of imperial terror that
was meant to publicly demonstrate Roman supremacy,
the cross epitomized the fate of all enemies of Rome. Crucifixion was the supreme penalty and was not used spar-
ingly, especially on the Jewish people. Tens of thousands
would breathe their last while on public display, hanging
on a Roman cross.[13]

Once under the thumb of Rome, Caesar took charge
of Israel's political future. Antipater was appointed as the

---

[12] Israel effectively ended her independence when Hyracanus II joined
forces with Pompey in 63 BC. Pompey entered the temple and rein-
stated Hyracanus as the high priest.

[13] Josephus, *The Complete Works*, 722, 736, 739.

procurator of Judea. His coronation began a royal line that lasted for nearly a century. His son, Herod the Great, came to power by living in the full embrace of Rome. He refused nothing Rome offered. To establish his kingship in the sight of his Jewish countrymen, he razed the temple built by Zerubbabel and constructed a new one in its place. The new temple was adorned with all the riches and pomp of Rome's wealth. While Herod's magnificent temple was the crown of Israel, there was no doubt that his administration was unflinchingly loyal to Roman interests. No matter how he tried, he could never win the hearts of his Jewish subjects.

But it wasn't only the politicians in Israel who were puppets of Rome; the chief priests in the temple were corrupt too. Herod's splendid temple was staffed by spiritual employees whose positions and paychecks were endorsed by Rome. Revenues generated by the temple in Jerusalem were taxed heavily. The money that was exchanged for official temple currency and the sacrificial animals bought and sold in its courts were profitable businesses whose proceeds went to Rome. The place of God's name and glory was generating lavish returns for the harlot. And it was all taking place under the auspices of the religious leaders of Jerusalem.

The religious life of the common Jew changed very little under the Romans. The Hellenistic tolerance that assimilated the surrounding pagan cultures was extended toward the Jewish people in Judea. As long as they remained obedient to Caesar, they were free to follow the religious traditions that had made them distinct as a nation. The benefits of friendship with Rome, combined with the dangers of disloyalty, made capitulation an easy choice. The political stability and economic prosperity that Rome offered to all who embraced her became a temptation that many Jews could not resist.

The Bonds of Rome

Deep darkness covered the land. The shadow of Rome's influence had been cast over the whole of Israel. The sinful influence of the city was having a devastating effect. Israel's subjugation wasn't merely political; it was spiritual. The nation was held captive to the demonic powers at work behind Rome and was suffering tremendous spiritual oppression. The demonic power emanating from Rome entangled many Jews in prostitution and witchcraft. Others turned to wine and lived as drunkards. The onslaught of demonic seduction ensnared the people of God, rich and poor alike. Satanic power afflicted them with paralysis, sickness, and masochistic insanity. The dark forces of hell were on a full-scale advance.

There was only one possible answer to Rome's unbending oppression. A king like Zerubbabel was needed to deliver Israel from her enemies. But King Herod was on the throne and he was no Zerubbabel. A high priest like Joshua was needed for the temple to be restored and dedicated to God. But even Zerubbabel and Joshua still wouldn't be enough; only a hero greater than Moses and David could lead the Jewish people out of this captivity. Caesar's empire dwarfed ancient Egypt in every way and was far greater than any enemy King David ever conquered. The empire was too strong and the leadership in Israel too compromised. Every human attempt to expel the Romans ended in mass crucifixion. There was only one hope for all of Israel. The hope of every faithful Jew rested fully on the promised Messiah.

God had promised that He would send a deliverer to Israel in her darkest hour. This promised king was coming to permanently disarm the power of Israel's oppressors and establish an unending kingdom with a fully restored house of prayer as its central feature. The Law, the Prophets, and the Writings all testified of His imminent appearing. Abraham, Moses, David, Isaiah, and many others in the Hebrew Scriptures prophesied that the coming Messiah would fulfill every promise God had given to Israel. The promised Messiah was Israel's only hope of ending her captivity.

There was no end to the number of charlatans and deceivers who took advantage of Israel's messianic expectancies. Many claimed to be the promised one. Some posed as prophets. Others promised to lead military campaigns against the Romans. But the Jewish leaders in Jerusalem weren't about to forfeit their positions of power to rogue commoners posing as the long-awaited Messiah. The fate of these small uprisings was always the same—failure. These were days of tremendous upheaval in Israel.

But the faithful were waiting patiently for God to break the pagan oppression of Rome. Never taking up arms or inspiring rebellions, the saints understood that the nation was under a dark power and that only divine intervention could destroy. Faithful friends of the Lord were partnering with Him in prayer—intercessors like Anna, who served God in fasting and prayer for the redemption of Jerusalem. She gave her entire life to partnering with God in intercession, praying day and night until the Messiah came to Jerusalem (Lk. 2:36–38). Anna was one among a hidden army who travailed in the secret place. And while the faithful cried out, God was preparing to break into the earth in a way that no one but He had imagined.[14]

---

[14] Eph. 3:4.

TEN
JACOB'S LADDER

Truly, truly, I say to you, you will see heaven opened, and the angels of God ascending and descending on the Son of Man.

—John 1:51

WORD REACHED KING HEROD'S COURT of some foreigners from the east stirring up a controversy in Jerusalem. Herod had heard numerous rumors of men claiming to be the Messiah, but something about this particular report was different. These were foreigners who shouldn't know about Israel's promised king. This was different indeed. Three men had made a long journey to Jerusalem to search out an ancient prophecy. A star had mysteriously risen in the night sky that foretold the birth of the long-awaited king of Israel. When Herod heard that foreigners were asking about the birth of the Messiah, he became deeply troubled. The birth of the Messiah meant only one thing to Herod: the end of his royal line.

All of Jerusalem was troubled by this news. Could it be? Was the Messiah born? Was Israel's deliverance finally at hand? One thing was sure: Herod wasn't going to wait to find out. He quickly assembled the chief priests and scribes in order to ascertain where it was prophesied the Messiah would be born. With every intention of murdering the infant Messiah, Herod sent the wise men to Bethlehem to locate the newborn king of Israel.

Finally they arrived in Bethlehem to find what they had come so far to see—the star was resting over a small house. When they entered, they came face to face with the greatest mystery ever conceived. The magnitude of their discovery overwhelmed them. There was only one response. Each fell prostrate before the baby. This wasn't a ritual show of veneration; it was wholehearted worship!

The Incarnation

Before the world began, God ordained an event upon which all creation would hinge. Just as light first infused the created realm with a single divine utterance, now the ultimate light of heaven had come through God's final word. The one and only eternal Son of God had stepped down from heaven into time and space to take on the form of an infant. The fullness of God had come to dwell bodily in a beautiful, helpless, cooing baby. He was the "Bethel" that Jacob had seen in his dream, the point of contact between heaven and earth. The bridge between the heavenly and earthly realm wasn't a ladder—it was a human being. The gateway of heaven had become flesh. The greatest mystery that had been hidden from the beginning was at hand.

God's eternal plan to unite the heavenly and earthly realms was initiated in the incarnation of Jesus Christ. Jesus was, at the same time, both fully God and fully human: the embodiment of God's plan to reunite heaven and earth in a shared reality. Heaven and earth had come together in the God-man. The divorce that occurred when Adam first embraced sin had no human remedy. Only One could heal the separation between heaven and earth. And now the King of heaven had come.

The intercession of Christ was the only way that the kingdom of heaven could come to sinful men. Without a sinless mediator, there was no way for a holy God to fellowship with sinful humans. When Adam fell, he joined Satan's cosmic rebellion. Because of Adam, the entire human race was hostile to God and enemies to God's purpose in the earth. But now Christ had come as humanity's sole mediator, to stand in the gap between God and men.

In fact, every relationship that the holy God of heaven had and would have with sinful humans in the past or future was possible through the intercession of Christ. Ever since the garden of Eden, God had ordained that His government would be implemented through partnership with humans. Noah, Abraham, Moses, and David had all partnered with God through intercession as He extended His blessings to others. In Jesus, God Himself became the ultimate intercessor.[1] The partnership of God the Father with God the Son in the form of a human brought the kingdom of God back to earth. Not since the garden of Eden had the Creator so communed with creation. Once again God walked among us.

For thirty years Jesus lived in utter obscurity. Only a few knew His true identity. He lived in perfect obedience to

---

[1] Intercession is the reality of human beings partnering with God in releasing His government into the earth. Standing in the gap is standing in partnership with God on behalf of others in order that His will be done on earth as it is in heaven. This partnership has many expressions (e.g., prayer, preaching, singing, etc.), but can only take place through Jesus by the Holy Spirit.

His Father's will and patiently awaited His unveiling to the world. He lived in Israel during the nation's greatest period of uncertainty. He saw His Jewish countrymen under the heavy yoke of Rome. He saw the oppression growing in the land. He well knew the dire circumstances of His fellow Jews.

But more importantly, Jesus understood the real power behind the evils of the Roman Empire. To defeat Israel's true enemy meant striking a death blow to mankind's most ancient foe. This primordial enemy had been seducing humans to rebel against God since the beginning, working to bring all of mankind into darkness. The true king of Babylon wasn't Caesar; it was Satan. His temptation always came with the same tagline: progression, utopia, to make a name, to become as God. Sin and death were his most intimate allies. Satan was at work once again through the power of Rome. And many of the leaders in Israel had already welcomed his dark power.

Kingdoms Collide

> And the devil took him up and showed Him all the kingdoms of the world in a moment of time, and said to Him, "To you I will give all this authority and their glory, for it has been delivered to me, and I give it to whom I will."
>
> —Luke 4:5

Nimrod gave his life in pursuit of power. Nebuchadnezzar became so intoxicated with the desire for personal glory that God struck his mind with insanity. The pursuit of human power and glory in agreement with the kingdom of darkness was the foundation stone of the city of Babylon. Now Satan was nearly ready to unleash his tyrannical leadership in Rome. He was looking for the perfect human candidate to assume the role of Caesar and, in direct partnership, rule the earth from Rome.[2] This is the role he was offering to Jesus.

It was true, or at least partly true. Satan really had been given authority over the kingdoms of the world. However, this authority had not been given by God. In fact, God had never given Satan authority over anything. Satan's authority had come through Adam—Adam's sin to be more precise. Adam was to rule the earth and steward it in loving partnership with God. But when he sinned, Adam broke off all relationship with God and joined Satan's rebellion. All in Adam's line had since been completely given over to the direction of an evil taskmaster. And Satan wasn't about to loosen his grip over the human race now.

There it was: Satan's final temptation. Near the point of death, gaunt, exhausted, struggling just to walk, Jesus had fasted His way through the Judean wilderness for forty days. Now all He had to do was bow the knee—simply give in and accept the offer. It was the path that so many had followed before, a temptation no mortal had been able to resist. The glory of Rome and the entire world was at His fingertips. His suffering could all be over. All Jesus had to do was indulge a little compromise.

But with a blaze of holy fire in His eyes, Jesus looked the devil straight in the eye. Suddenly the tables turned. Satan began to tremble. He remembered that look. It was the same look of fury that had forever banished him from heaven. It was the same zeal. It was the same fire. Satan's worst fears had been realized; the King had come to reclaim the earth!

[2] Satan's offer to rule the kingdoms of the earth must be understood as an offer to become the emperor of Rome. Rome was the sole world power at the time his offer was being made.

Be gone, Satan! For it is written, "You shall worship the Lord your God and him only shall you
serve."

—Matthew 4:8

The Return from Captivity

With that, the King emerged from the desert. Where the
first Adam had failed, the last Adam had overcome. Where
the nation of Israel had fallen short of the promise only to
wander the desert for forty years, Christ had conquered
in forty days. Now He had come to lead His people out of
exile. As Zerubbabel had led the returning captives back
to Israel, Jesus was now calling all those held captive to
the new Babylon to return to the ultimate promised land.

From that time Jesus began to preach, saying,
"Repent, for the kingdom of heaven is at hand."
—Matthew 4:17

This return from captivity transcended Israel and Rome.
It wasn't just the Jewish people who lived as exiles. Even
the Romans themselves were exiles. They just didn't know
it. In fact, people from every nation, tribe, and language all
shared the same status as exiles.

Long before Israel was a nation, another exile trans-
pired that shaped all of human existence. When Adam and
Eve ate of the forbidden fruit, the entrance of sin changed
everything. Adam had once fellowshipped with God freely
without shame; now he lived in hiding from God. He had
once enjoyed the prospect of living forever, now death was
inescapable. Once humans had lived in the perfect para-
dise that God intended; now they had been driven from
the garden of Eden only to live as exiles.

He has sent me to proclaim liberty to the captives and recovering of sight to the blind, to set
at liberty those who are oppressed.
—Luke 4:18

Jesus had come to lead all exiles out of captivity. Not just the captives in Israel, but every exile from Eden as well. Now the time had come for the human race—all those who had been driven from Eden—to return home. From those who had been blinded by the devil's lies to those who were bound by the chains of sin, liberty had come at last!

The Rock of Offense

Like Zerubbabel, Jesus was a king with no earthly title. He was a man with a royal bloodline but with no reputation. He had no ties to Herod's court but had every right to rule it as Israel's true king. In fact, Jesus was a descendant of Zerubbabel. And that meant he was also a true descendant of King David. In other words, Jesus was the rightful heir to the throne of Israel just as Zerubbabel had been. But now there was an imposter on the throne by the name of Herod: a charlatan who was put into place by the New Babylon.

Jesus was the promised Messiah, but He was not what Israel expected. The Jewish people envisioned the Messiah garnering his forces like mighty King David. They imagined that He would be divinely empowered to establish Israel's rule over the nations just as God had promised. But Jesus was about to offend everyone whose hope was anchored in the present age. The coming offense arose from a fundamental misunderstanding of the kingdom of heaven. The nation of Israel did not recognize Jesus and were offended at Him because He had not come to throw off the yoke of Rome.

Just as it had been in the garden of Eden, humans would be given the right to freely choose obedience. King Jesus would not settle for anything less than loving devotion to His royal rule. The kind of love He was after could never be coerced. The King of heaven had come to freely offer Himself for mankind. Although He was the commander of the most powerful army in the universe, He would not take the world by force. The question before the world was: who would bow before the King of heaven, who came not as a mighty conqueror but as the humble servant of all?

But on the other hand, the Jewish expectation of a conquering Messiah wasn't totally erroneous either. The Hebrew Scriptures clearly promised a day when the kingdom of heaven would come with force. A Jewish king would, in fact, come upon an unsuspecting world to bring it under submission with a rod of iron. A day would come when the full power of heaven's army of angelic warriors would be unleashed, but it would not come until the world had had an opportunity to choose its allegiance. Everyone on earth had an eternal choice to make, an unending citizenship to claim.

Herod's Temple

> It is written, "My house shall be a house of prayer,"
> but you have made it a den of robbers."
> —Luke 19:46

The chief priests were furious. "By what authority could He do this?" they asked. They were the ones with the backing of Rome. They had charge of everything in the temple. From the sacrifices to the currency exchange, the chief priests had the final say over it all. Now this upstart from Nazareth had just demolished the central core of commerce in the temple? They were outraged. Only Israel's high priest possessed this kind of executive authority.

That was exactly Jesus' point. He not only came as Israel's king, but He had come as her High Priest as well. Jesus entered the temple in Jerusalem and looked about the place that was supposed to be the house of God—a place of prayer for all nations, the seat of God's presence and glory—but found instead that the temple had become another victim of the harlot's global network of commerce and false religion. The temple required cleansing, and as the High Priest, it was Jesus' job to do it. Consumed by zeal for His Father's house, Jesus brandished a whip and drove out all those who had set up businesses in the temple courts.

Returning from captivity not only meant an invitation to the kingdom of heaven, it also meant a new temple. The Hebrew prophets pointed to a day when the Messiah would come to build the true temple, a temple that would never fade away. That is exactly what Jesus had come to do as the High Priest. But the temple Jesus had in mind was far greater than the spectacle Herod had built.

> I tell you, something greater than the temple is
> here.
>
> —Matthew 12:6

The True Temple

Herod the Great spent decades pouring the riches of Rome into adorning the temple. It had no need of physical repair. All of the prescribed rituals were in place. There was no need for a change in its daily operation. The priesthood was fully staffed. There was no need to hire anyone. But nonetheless, Jesus had come to build the temple. Just as

Joshua had joined Zerubbabel to rebuild the temple in the days after the Babylonian captivity, Jesus had come to call His people out of captivity to rebuild the true temple in the days of Rome.

But this temple wasn't made of stones. Jesus was an architect of another sort. The temple He had in mind was to be constructed out of human beings in restored relationship with God. Jesus called to the rich and the poor, male and female, Jew and Gentile. All who were held under the bondage of the evil one were invited. Prostitutes, tax collectors, drunkards; now was the time to break all allegiance to Babylon and follow Jesus to the promised land. Anyone who would listen and follow could become a living, breathing stone in Jesus' temple. Out of these pieces of building material, Jesus would build His Church.

No longer would the people of God be restricted to the Jewish nation; they would be defined by faith in the Messiah. The Church would in no way replace Israel as the people of God; rather, Israel was given the first invitation to respond to her Messiah. This gloriously good news found exclusively through faith in Christ was offered to the Jew first, but was not limited to the Jewish people; it extended beyond all ethnic and gender boundaries, to all who would respond in repentance and faith. The stones of God's house were to be made up of believers of all races and nations, for the dwelling place of God was to be amongst His people.

This was God's promise through the prophets of the Old Testament. The Church itself, comprised of Jew and Gentile alike, would be the house of the Lord. Just as the temple had been the place where the presence of God dwelt, now the Church was the Bethel of God.

> So then you are no longer strangers and aliens,
> but you are fellow citizens with the saints and
> members of the household of God, built on the
> foundation of the apostles and prophets, Christ
> Jesus himself being the cornerstone, in whom
> the whole structure, being joined together,
> grows into a holy temple in the Lord.
>
> —Ephesians 2:19–21

To build this temple, Jesus began the work of laying its foundation. He chose a group of Jewish men who would serve as the foundation of the Church. His unmatched leadership transformed a ragtag group of fishermen and tax collectors into apostolic bedrock. They were to become pillars in the first generation of Christians. But before this rowdy crew would turn the world upside down as mighty apostles, they would first be refined with fire.

Jesus was the chief builder of the temple, but He was also its cornerstone. Every one of the billions of souls saved throughout the Church age would find a foundation in His person. His name was salvation. His faithfulness sealed the new covenant. His teaching was the truth that would light the way for the Church. His Spirit was the power to accomplish the will of God. The first stone to be laid was the cornerstone. The stone on which every other stone would be built upon was Jesus Christ Himself, in every way the preeminent One.

Just as in the days of Nebuchadnezzar, Israel was in exile. As the new embodiment of Babylon, first-century Rome held Israel captive. But the captivity went far beyond the power of Caesar. It extended to the true king of Babylon himself, who had successfully driven the entire human race into exile from Eden and bound the descendants of

Adam in darkness. But now the promised Messiah had come. As High Priest and King, Jesus had come to Israel to lead His people out of captivity, and into the promised land to rebuild the house of prayer. Now the same question that had faced the generation of Joshua and Zerubbabel hundreds of years before was presented once again: who would break allegiance with Babylon and return to the promised land?

Rendering unto Caesar

> Is it lawful for us to give tribute to Caesar, or not?
>
> —Luke 20:22

It was a stroke of sinister genius. One question would by its very nature necessarily offend either the Jewish people or the Romans. Should a God-fearing Jew pay taxes to Rome or not? Or to put it in another way, was it right to willingly give money to the king of Babylon? They took advantage of an impossible dilemma. If Jesus were to answer yes, He would be seen as a puppet of Caesar, discredited among faithful Jews. If He said no to please Jewish anti-Rome sentiment, He would become a clear target for Roman authorities.

The scribes and the chief priests were fully aware of Jesus' growing popularity. There was no way to deny it. Jesus' following was gaining strength and threatening their power and influence over the people. Their concern led to outright conspiracy. They planned to catch Him, accuse Him, and have Him murdered. To do this, they set up a trap that would expose Jesus as being either a threat or a puppet of Rome. If the Roman-endorsed spiritual leadership in Jerusalem could prove that Jesus was a threat to Rome, they knew how to pull the right strings to have Him capitally punished. On the other hand, if they could prove that Jesus was compromised by Roman interests, as they themselves were, they could discredit Him in the sight of the people.

> Render to Caesar the things that are Caesar's,
> and to God the things that are God's.
> —Luke 20:25

His perfect wisdom silenced them all. This answer not only addressed their trickery, it held far-reaching implications for the faithful living in subjection to Babylon. Not only should Jews give their taxes to Caesar, they should also give everything else rightfully due to Rome as well. Jesus was laying the foundation for the surprising New Testament teaching on how to live in Babylon, and that foundation was submission.[3]

Even though corrupt, Rome was still a government instituted by God and was to be regarded as such. As difficult as it was to believe, God had put Rome in its place. His teaching answered the issue holistically. Caesar was a human being in charge of a human government that offered services to its subjects. The Roman government built and maintained roads in the region, and its military force afforded citizens protection and stability. Living under the protection and provision of Rome had requirements: paying taxes, obeying laws, and, in general, being a good citizen

---

[3] This teaching is repeatedly addressed throughout the New Testament by the apostles who lived in the Roman Empire. In Romans 13:1, Paul writes by the Holy Spirit, "Let every person be subject to the governing authorities. For there is no authority except from God, and those that exist have been instituted by God." Laws that govern taxation, crime, business, and other ordinances that give order to a civilization should be obeyed as due to Caesar (Rom. 13:7). This letter was written to Christians living in Rome who would later suffer fiercely from Roman persecutions.

of the empire.

But that wasn't the entire story. Rome wasn't simply a human city with a human government; a spiritual reality lurked behind the human level. Demonic forces were often at work behind Caesar's motivations. When the edicts of Caesar did not align with the kingdom of God as revealed through the Word of God, immediate and unbending allegiance to God was required.[4] Even if Rome overstepped its authority and demanded an allegiance that belonged only to God, the believer was commanded to obey God no matter the cost.

The Hour of Darkness

Jesus' wisdom shocked the chief priests and scribes into quiet awe. Their efforts to defame Him backfired. They were losing face to a man with no credentials, who was hailed by many as the king of the Jewish people. Their fear for their positions turned to panic. They could turn to only one power for help now. They began seeking ways to turn Him over to Rome.

> And they weighed out as my wages thirty pieces of silver . . . the lordly price at which I was priced by them.
>
> —Zechariah 11:12–13

It wasn't one of the corrupt priests. It wasn't Herod. It wasn't even a Roman. In the greatest betrayal in history, one of Jesus' own disciples turned Him in. Maybe it was because Jesus had no plan to take Jerusalem by force.

---

[4] In Acts 4:19, the apostles Peter and John proclaimed this truth to the scribes and elders who had strictly prohibited the preaching of Jesus in Jerusalem when they said, "Whether it is right in the sight of God to listen to you rather than to God, you must judge."

Maybe it was because the love of money had so infiltrated his affections that thirty pieces of silver were enough to perpetrate treason. Whatever it was, Judas had surrendered his heart to the prince of darkness.

Satan had long been trying to kill Jesus. Ever since his defeat in the wilderness, it was apparent that Jesus had come to destroy everything the devil worked so hard to build. For thousands of years, Satan successfully bound humans in sin. His demonic army was on a full-scale advance in Israel until Jesus came. Now nothing was sure. The foundations of hell were being shaken. There was no demon that Jesus could not cast out. Even sin and death, Satan's greatest allies, were threatened. Jesus was forgiving sin and raising the dead! There was only one possible way to prevail. His rebellion against the King of heaven failed once, but this was a whole new battlefield. This wasn't heaven, it was the earth, and the entire human race had already joined his rebellion. Now it was time to gather his troops and bring the kingdom of heaven to an end.

No King but Caesar

In one of the greatest cosmic ironies ever to unfold, the High King of heaven, the Judge of all the earth, was on trial. The One who would one day judge every soul ever created stood before a human judge, accused of blasphemy, and was convicted in that farcical courtroom. The people turned their only hope for heaven over to the Roman governor, Pontius Pilate. Jesus stood intentionally silent before His accusers. The Lamb of God was being led to the altar.

Having found no fault in Jesus, Pilate wanted to flog and release Him, but the cruelty of Pilate was deemed too merciful by the chief priests and elders. The leadership in

Jerusalem would accept nothing less than the application of Rome's most cruel punishment. They stirred up the
crowds into a vicious rage. "Crucify Him!" they cried. Pilate
tried to resist their murderous request, but they knew the
one way to coerce the spineless governor. Israel's leaders
had so fully embraced Rome that they used their own allegiance to the king of Babylon as leverage against Pilate,
questioning, in fact, his own loyalty.

> If you release this man, you are not Caesar's
> friend. Everyone who makes himself a king op-
> poses Caesar.
>
> —John 19:12

> Pilate said to them, "Shall I crucify your King?"
> The chief priests answered, "We have no king
> but Caesar."
>
> —John 19:15b–16

It was nothing less than a pledge of allegiance to the
king of Babylon. The Jewish leadership made their choice
to stand in full agreement with the great harlot. They had
become the God-defying builders of Babel. They preferred
connection with the political power of Babylon to the return from exile that was occurring through the promised
Messiah. Their defiance against God brought to light what
was kept obscure by their religious forms—they had fully
embraced the satanic spirit of Babylon. And because they
rejected God as their king, soon God would give them a
Caesar after their own hearts.

The Gateway of God

Crucifixion was the execution method Rome adopted to
put on public display those who dared oppose its power.

The crucifixion spectacle was designed to inspire allegiance to Rome, to be a symbol that created terror at the thought of disloyalty. But in the very symbol of the strength and power of Rome, every demonic power and principality would suffer a fatal blow. God sent His Son into the world to die on a Roman cross.

> He disarmed the rulers and authorities and put
> them to open shame, by triumphing over them
> in [the cross.]
>   —Colossians 2:15

Jesus was put on public display. But it was a display that only God could truly see. The eyes of men and demons couldn't perceive what was happening. Crucifixions had become so common that no one flinched at the sight anymore. Many Jews had suffered the same fate. To the eyes of men and demons, it seemed like just another display of Roman supremacy. But God saw the display entirely differently. In the cross, Jesus disarmed every dark power and put them to open shame. The cross of Jesus Christ wasn't defeat; it was the very triumph of God!

In all the fury and brutality that Rome could pour out on those who opposed Caesar, Jesus absorbed the wrath of God. The scourging, the crown of thorns, the spitting, the cursing, the nakedness, the nails, the slow agonizing bleeding and suffocating to death—in one glorious act, God demonstrated His perfect justice in judging sin and, at the same time, displayed His glorious mercy in providing a perfect sacrifice for sinners. The flawless One suffered a death that only a sinner rightfully deserved. The One who never sinned became sin on the cross, that all those who believe in Him might become the righteousness of God (2 Cor. 5:21). The cross of Jesus Christ rendered sin powerless and death's sting impotent.

Through the cross, the true "gateway of God" was opened to earth. It could never have happened any other way. Every misguided attempt of man to reach into heaven and make a name for himself was confusion. Only God could bridge the impassable chasm that Adam's sin had forged. The gateway to God was fully opened through the cross of Jesus Christ.

> That he might be the firstborn among many brothers.
>
> —Romans 8:29

The chief priests could not stop Him. Rome could not stop Him. Satan could not stop Him. Even death itself could not hold Him! Jesus Christ was the first human ever to enter eternity in resurrection. But He wouldn't be the last. He had come to lead His people out of exile. Now He was the first to step across the threshold into the promised land. The resurrected Christ was the last Adam; the sole representative of what the human race was supposed to be. God the Son, in the form of a man, partnered with God the Father and accomplished for fallen humans what no one could have dreamed.

ELEVEN

THE FIRES OF BABYLON

WITH THE ADVENT OF THE CHURCH, a whole new breed of strangers in Babylon was born. And just as in the days of Zerubbabel, every captive who desired to follow the king to the city of God had to first leave Babylon. God had birthed the Church in Babylonian captivity. The first Christians lived their entire lives in subjection to Rome. The apostles and the churches they established were all within the scope and rule of Caesar. They knew what it was to live in a culture utterly given over to sexual perversion and idolatry.

The teachings of Jesus laid the foundation for how the Church would overcome in Babylon. Christ never taught His disciples to take up arms in revolutionary zealotry.[1] Jesus foretold the coming destruction of Jerusalem and

---

[1] Many in Judea felt that God couldn't possibly want His people subject to pagan power. Jewish zealots took up arms and sabotaged the Romans in order to liberate Judea from Rome. The Jewish War and the mass suicide of Jews at Masada were the climax of the anti-Roman Jewish nationalism. This is not a blanket endorsement of Christian pacifism. We in America are grateful for the great sacrifices that have been made to defend the liberties of our great republic—freedom must forever be defended from tyranny.

instructed His disciples to leave the city. They were specifically admonished not to fight but to flee, because this destruction was not merely the wrath of Rome but the wrath of God. The New Testament had an entirely different method of combating the spirit and power of Babylon, and it didn't include physical violence. Through the leading of the apostles and guidance of the Holy Spirit, the Church adopted the only way to overcome the power of the spirit of Babylon—through partnership with God in intercession.

> First of all, then, I urge that supplications, prayers, intercessions, and thanksgivings be made for all people, for kings and all who are in high positions, that we may lead a peaceful and quiet life, godly and dignified in every way. This is good, and it is pleasing in the sight of God our Savior, who desires all people to be saved and to come to the knowledge of the truth.
>
> —1 Timothy 2:1–4

The apostle Paul understood the correlation between fervent prayer and living a peaceful life under Roman rule. As Jeremiah told those going into Babylonian captivity to seek the good of the city, Paul commanded Christians to pray for rulers in the Roman hierarchy so that they might live peaceable lives in godliness. Intercession was the God-ordained way of releasing His power. Only in response to the prayers of His people would God release the angels of heaven and bind demonic power.

Tolerating Jezebel

The early church was plagued by the influence of Rome. Many of the congregations were seduced by compromise.

Wolves and false teachers led the people of God astray with false religion. Demonic doctrines like syncretism, Gnosticism, and legalism were all consigned to shipwreck the faith of the Church.

> I know your works, your love and faith and ser-
> vice and patient endurance, and that your latter
> works exceed the first. But I have this against
> you, that you tolerate that woman Jezebel, who
> calls herself a prophetess and is teaching and
> seducing my servants to practice sexual immo-
> rality and to eat food sacrificed to idols.
> —Revelation 2:19–20

The Church was in a constant battle against the influence of Roman culture. In Thyatira, a false prophetess was seducing believers to commit acts of sexual immorality and idolatry. But the Lord permitted no place for compromise. He warned of severe judgment on the woman who introduced the ways of Babylon and those who compromised with her. The Lord admonished them to repent and set their hearts toward wholehearted obedience. There was no place for the darkness of Rome within the sacred dwelling of the Church. To keep her free from spiritual drunkenness, Jesus taught His disciples, "Stay awake at all times, praying that you have strength to escape all these things that are going to take place, and to stand before the Son of Man" (Lk. 21:36).

There was only one way to guard their hearts and stay free from debauchery and drunkenness (the effects of Babylon): the Church had to remain vigilant in prayer. This meant that the Church was to be both aware of the imminence of Jesus' second coming, and to remain constant in prayer.

Jesus required that His people be informed of the events of the end times. He commanded alertness and awareness so that they might endure the "what must take place" (Rev. 4:1). The combination of understanding God's end-time plans and operating in the ministry of intercession would keep the Church's heart free from the spiritual confusion and moral compromise of Roman culture. Jesus taught His disciples that temptation could only be overcome through prayer (Mt. 26:41). Through prayer, human weakness embraces the all-sufficient strength of God's grace. A life lived outside a spirit of prayer is a life lived by the flesh, a life void of power to overcome the temptations of Babylon.

To those who overcame the decadent influence of the harlot and lived free of compromise with her, Jesus promised world dominion.

> The one who conquers and who keeps my works until the end, to him I will give authority over the nations, and he will rule them with a rod of iron ... even as I myself have received authority from my Father.
>
> —Revelation 2:26–27

Though the prophetess Jezebel had introduced sexual immorality and idolatry to its members, the Lord still presented an eternal promise to the church in Thyatira. Those who compromised with the harlot would be judged, but those who overcame her idolatry and immorality and lived in partnership with Him by the power of the Spirit would rule the nations with Christ.

The Winds of Change

> Children, it is the last hour, and as you have heard that antichrist is coming, so now many

antichrists have come. Therefore we know that
it is the last hour.

—1 John 2:18

As the Holy Spirit empowered the apostles to establish the Church, it wasn't long before the winds of political change began to blow in Rome. Rome's tolerance of Judaism and Christianity began to fade, and storm clouds of tyranny formed on the horizon. Behind the licentious face of "tolerance" awaited a hidden malice. The people of Rome were well prepared for the next step in Satan's design. Deluded by sexual immorality and idolatry, the masses would have no conviction or discernment to resist the antichrist power, a power that would lead them to the brink of annihilation.

The first indication that change was on the horizon of imperial Rome was the arrival of Caesar Gaius (Caligula). Having gained popularity because of his benevolence and affable etiquette, Caligula became severely ill, even to the very threshold of death. From the moment he escaped the perilous gulf of mortality, something seized him, twisting his mind and perverting his desires. The antichrist spirit so consumed his mind that he believed he was immortal, sat in temples around the empire, and dressed as one of the gods. Unlike Caesars before him, Caligula asserted his own divinity by calling himself the brother of the highest of the pagan gods, Jupiter.[2] He ordered the building of temples and altars in veneration of himself.

Caligula ignored the freedoms previously afforded the Jewish people, and when he discovered that they refused to set up his image in the temple, he was outraged. If the Jewish people would not willingly worship him, he

[2]   Josephus, *The Complete Works*, 603.

was prepared to invoke worship by force.[3] He ordered his general to invade Judea and set up his image in the temple. But when the Roman general saw that the Jewish people would willingly die without a fight before they allowed Caligula's image into the temple, he appealed to Caligula to relent from his demand and avert the unnecessary bloodshed. This appeal did nothing but further infuriate the emperor, but before action could be taken against his general, Caligula was assassinated in a political plot.

Though Caligula would not see his wicked schemes against God's people fulfilled, his blasphemous autocracy was the beginning of the shift in Roman policy that would replace the licentiousness of Hellenism with tyrannical intolerance. The antichrist spirit was set to dominate Rome.

But calm came before the storm and a certain sense of normalcy and freedom returned to Israel for a season after Caligula was assassinated. The next Caesar, Claudius, was nowhere near as self-obsessed as his predecessor but the reprieve under Claudius would not last long.

During his reign, Claudius married the sister of Caligula, Agrippina. Roman law had to be changed to allow for the incestuous union, for besides being Caligula's sister, Agrippina was also Claudius's niece. However, from the day of her marriage, Agrippina reserved an adulterous

---

[3] Though the apostate Jewish leadership was entirely compromised by the harlot spirit of Rome, they would never bow to the antichrist power that was arising. The Jews were unbendingly monotheistic and strictly against offering worship to any other god, including the emperor worship that was generally practiced by other Roman subjects. Under the religious tolerance of Rome, Caesar had allowed the Jews the freedom to practice their religion as they pleased. Because Caesar's primary interest was to keep the empire under control and the Jewish people were so strongly opposed to the pagan practices of Rome, they had been allowed to make sacrifices on Caesar's behalf rather than offering him direct divine honor.

lover. During the marriage, she continually worked behind the scenes to secure her young son's destiny as emperor.[4] Claudius may have been the emperor in title, but just as Queen Jezebel ruled through Ahab, no one doubted that Agrippina ruled Rome from behind the throne.

The New Apollo

When Agrippina's son became old enough to take power, Claudius was the only thing standing between her and absolute control of Rome. In her lust for power, Claudius' murder was conceived and the emperor was poisoned.[5] At his death, Agrippina moved quickly to transition full power to her son. His ascent to the throne began an entirely new order of emperor. The people of Rome met the arrival of Lucius Domitius Ahenobarbus in AD 54 with great optimism. The masses firmly believed that this new Caesar would usher in an age of hope. But the quirky eccentricities that at first amused and entertained the public would in the end turn into raving insanity, leaving the empire in fearful chaos. The adoptive name of the new emperor was Nero.[6]

Agrippina thought that securing the throne for her son would fortify her own power, but she soon realized that her influence had been incapacitated. As a young man, Nero spurned his mother's political power plays and began to understand his position of unrivaled power. He followed in

[4] Nero was adopted by Claudius.

[5] Taking into consideration Agrippina's murderous desire for power and the odd coincidence that Claudius died when Nero was just old enough to rule, not to mention the well-orchestrated transition of power, there can be little doubt that Agrippina was guilty of murdering her husband.

[6] This Caesar would most closely prefigure the eschatological Antichrist.

the footsteps of his mother's political shrewdness. When it became clear that Nero would not serve Agrippina's political interests, she threatened to support his stepbrother's claim to the throne.[7]

Nero caught wind of the conspiracy in time and acted quickly. Before Agrippina was able to succeed in her coup, Nero eliminated his greatest political threat with poison. He then severed any further opportunity Agrippina might have had at forming political alliances against him by assigning her to a separate residence.

As Nero's power grew, so did his vices. Believing that supporting the Roman senate would be unprofitable, he dissolved their powers. Not even the once mighty senate would have any influence on Nero's decisions. With no one to answer to, Nero abandoned himself to the growing evil of his heart. He frequented brothels and taverns with his friends. He roamed the streets of Rome in disguise, stole from stores like a petty thief, and assaulted wayfarers like a common thug. In one moment of drunkenness, a rowdy friend quoted a Greek tragedy, shouting, "When I am dead, may the earth be overwhelmed by fire!" To which Nero replied with a grin, "While I am alive!"[8]

Agrippina's final grasp for power would lead to her ultimate undoing. Recognizing the growing power of Nero's lusts, she employed a last-ditch effort to regain her political power—she used her beauty in an incestuous attempt to seduce her own son. Nero was so blinded by his own lusts that only the protection of his political allies staved

[7] She let the emperor hear her say that Britannicus was grown up and was the true and worthy heir of his father's supreme position—now held, she added, by an adopted intruder, who used it to maltreat his mother. Tacitus, *The Annals of Imperial Rome, 290.*
[8] Champlin, *Nero*, 182. Exactly when and in what context this line of the Greek tragedy was amended by Nero is not given.

off Agrippina's advances.

Agrippina was too powerful to be left alive; through the advice of his counselors, Nero decided to kill his own mother. The men he sent surrounded her house. When they broke in, they found Agrippina awaiting her fate. A deathblow by sword pierced her womb. To Nero's other titles would now be added "the matricide."

After the murder of his mother, no iniquity was too evil for Nero. He kicked his pregnant wife to death in a fit of rage. To remedy his personal loss, he castrated and "married" a boy that reminded him of his murdered wife. In celebration of the basest of human lusts, his royal parties included common temple prostitutes and the highest-ranking officials of Rome. He devoted himself to satisfying every dark desire that hell could fill his heart with.[9] In giving himself over to unbridled demonic influences, Nero was becoming a beast.

Fully immersed in darkness, Nero began to believe that he was the "New Apollo," the incarnation of the sun god, the greatest expression of all human spiritual and physical achievement.[10] The same satanic lies that drove Nimrod and Nebuchadnezzar were now driving Nero stark raving mad. He installed his statue in Rome's temple of Mars and demanded to be worshiped. He commanded inscriptions be made referring to himself as "Almighty God" and "Savior."[11] Through Nero, the antichrist spirit had found an unhindered channel of satanic influence.

[9] "Nero was already corrupted by every lust, natural and unnatural." Tacitus, *The Annals of Imperial Rome*, 362.

[10] Champlin, *Nero*, 114.

[11] Sproul, *Last Days*, 188.

Neropolis

The new "Sun of Rome" dreamt of a golden city and the dawning of a golden age. Nero began to despise what he deemed the horrendous layout of Rome. He abhorred the poorly configured streets, and began to dream of a new city embellished in gold and boasting the most magnificent buildings in the world. His own palace, he imagined, would crown the city and feature a 120-foot statue of himself as the sun god. The new Rome would be renamed "Neropolis."[12] But before Rome could be rebuilt and bear his name, it first had to be destroyed. The city would soon know the destructive flames of its "New Apollo."

On a quiet mid-summer night, Rome was set ablaze. Menacing gangs roamed the streets, threatening any who dared to fight the flames. All except those who were causing the fires fled for their lives. The mighty city burned for over a week. While nearly the entire city was overwhelmed in fire, Nero was seen on his private stage singing of the destruction of Troy. Nothing so delighted his heart as the sight of Rome in flames.

As the knowledge of Nero's involvement came to light, public opinion turned against him. The fire served as a wakeup call to the citizens of Rome. Their spiritual drunkenness wore off, if but for a moment, as they turned their anger against Caesar. To divert public hatred and unite Romans under the banner of a similar interest, Nero blamed the growing number of Christians in Rome for the fire. It was a groundless accusation, but one quickly believed by the Roman mob who already hated Christians. The door opened for the fury of the antichrist to fall upon the people of God.

[12] "He [Nero] had decided to call Rome Neropolis." Tacitus, Epigraphs, as quoted in Champlin, Nero, 178.

The Gates of Hell

Christians were hated for their resistance to Roman influence. Considered atheists because they refused to worship the demon gods of Rome, they were criminalized because they would not compromise with the harlot spirit. They proclaimed a crucified Lord who was not Caesar; this, above all, infuriated Nero. The cross was supposed to be the symbol of Caesar's supremacy. Now it was being used to proclaim the supremacy of Christ!

When Christians were condemned for their participation in the Great Fire, they were found guilty not as incendiaries but as those who "hated the human race."[13] They refused to embrace the values and vision of Babylon and were made to suffer at the hands of those who did. As strangers in Babylon, the first Christians in Rome were criminalized for loving God's glory more than human glory.

In the face of fierce persecution, the early Christians preached Christ and did not shrink back from death. The grace and power of the Holy Spirit carried them through their darkest hour. Some were thrown to wild beasts; others were crucified or burned on stakes. Every execution was a public spectacle, a savage form of entertainment for the bloodthirsty crowds.

By standing firm in prayer, every faithful witness experienced God's power to endure. Jesus Himself manifested in His people, who withstood Satan's onslaught. The martyrs of that tribulation firmly understood that they were people of the resurrection; they would not compromise even in the face of death. Nero lit the long nights of that murderous persecution with lamps created from burning

13 Champlin, *Nero*, 121.

Christians. Both the apostle Peter and the apostle Paul were martyred during Nero's persecution.

> And they have conquered him by the blood of
> the Lamb and by the word of their testimony, for
> they loved not their lives even unto death.
> —Revelation 12:11

To follow the King to the promised land meant walking the same path He had walked. Death had lost its sting, but it still had to be faced. To walk the path of Jesus, one not only traveled through a physical death, but a daily dying to self. The cross was a requirement for any who wanted to follow Jesus, for the path to the promised land lay through the doorway of death.

Roman barbarity reached unprecedented levels as Nero inebriated the city with the blood of Christian martyrs. Yet after some time, even the deluded people of Rome eventually softened toward the Christians when it became apparent that the persecution had never been about the public good, but about satisfying Nero's insatiably savage bloodlust.[14]

The Roman policies of peace abroad were also quickly evolving into barbarity under Nero's leadership. His insane cruelty was reflected in the leaders he appointed to rule Judea. Under the yoke of their oppression, the Jewish people arose in rebellion against Rome. The escalation of this conflict infuriated Nero; he sent his general Titus Vespasian to march against Jerusalem and bring the Jewish nation into submission.

But Nero would never see the day when the Jewish insurrection would be quelled and the temple destroyed.

---

[14] Tacitus, *The Annals of Imperial Rome*, 366.

Before Jerusalem fell, the empire spiraled into financial and political chaos. Nero's fanatical spending and reckless tyranny had left Rome on the brink of bankruptcy. Before the empire had all but collapsed, Rome turned on Nero. The military defected and proclaimed others as emperor. The senate declared him a public enemy. As his imminent downfall approached, Nero tried to escape from Rome, but when he sought support, there was no one. Everyone loathed him. In the final hours before his suicide, Nero was abandoned by all.[15]

The Bethel of God

> "Who do you say that I am?" Simon Peter replied, "You are the Christ, the Son of the living God." And Jesus answered him, "Blessed are you, Simon Bar-Jonah! For flesh and blood has not revealed this to you, but my Father who is in heaven. And I tell you, you are Peter, and on this rock I will build my church, and the gates of hell shall not prevail against it."
>
> —Matthew 16:15–18

The foundations of the house of prayer had been laid. Led by the apostles and empowered by the Holy Spirit, the first generation of Christians endured the fires of Babylon. Centuries earlier, Zerubbabel and Joshua had led their generation out of Babylon back to Jerusalem to rebuild the temple. Now the kingdom of God had come to earth in the person of Jesus the Messiah. As the King, Jesus had come to bring the kingdom. As the High Priest, Jesus had come to build His temple.

[15] Nero's reign of terror came to an abrupt end with his suicide in AD 68.

The foundation had been laid, but there were yet many more stones to be set and many more fires to be endured. Other emperors would arise after Nero in the spirit of the antichrist, only to follow in his footsteps of persecution,[16] but the Church would carry on the mission she had been given. The more Rome tried to stamp out the fire, the more the fire spread. The gates of hell would never prevail. For thousands of years, the Church would advance the gospel of Jesus Christ.

The King had left the earth but had not left His people. As God's Bethel, the Church was the dwelling place of God in the earth. Within every single believer, Jesus Christ promised to take up residence through the Holy Spirit. His presence and glory lived on. From the right hand of power, Jesus continued to build His Church, knowing that the day would come when His temple would be finished (Mt. 28:18–20).

But before the temple would be ready for the return of Christ, the Church would undergo her greatest test. The greatest face-off between the saints and Babylon was not in the past but in the future. Rome fell from power over the centuries that followed, but Babylon would arise again. The first generation of Christians had been purified in the fires of Rome. The final generation would face the greatest challenge yet: Babylon the Great.

---

[16] Nero stood alone as the fullest picture of the eschatological Antichrist. Nero did not fulfill all of the criteria of the Antichrist prophecies, but he was, nonetheless, consumed by the spirit of antichrist. A good argument could be made that Nero was the Antichrist (see Sproul, *Last Days*, 186–189). However, when all of the biblical prophecies of the Antichrist are considered, Nero falls far short of the one who is yet to come. Nero did not set himself up to be worshiped in the temple (2 Thes. 2:4). Nero never had the technological ability to create a mark by which Roman citizens could participate in commerce (Rev. 13:16–17). Though he bore many marks of one consumed with the antichrist spirit, the list of reasons why Nero could not have been the ultimate Antichrist is far more convincing.

PART IV
THE PRELUDE

TWELVE

THE WINDS OF CHANGE

THE WORLD CAPITAL OF GERMANIA was still only a dream. For years, plans were crafted to transform Berlin into the greatest city in the world. The Führer himself had meticulously designed miniature models, sketches, and blueprints. These models were evidence of more than just a madman's pipedream. The same demonic vision of a golden city that had driven King Nebuchadnezzar and Caesar Nero was at work in another tyrant's mind. With help from his chief architect, Albert Speer, Adolf Hitler would soon roll out his plan to make Berlin the new world capital.

As the seat of Nazi power, Germania was slated to reign for a thousand years. The supreme city of the Reich would host the greatest architecture in the world. Among the magnificent architectural edifices Hitler had planned for Berlin was the Chancellery of the Reich and a victory arch that would dwarf the Arc de Triomphe in Paris. But the crowning glory of Germania would be the Great Hall. Designed to accommodate 180,000 people, the Great Hall would be capped with a massive dome that would have loomed over 700 feet tall and 800 feet in diameter.

Beneath the immaculate architecture was a sinister ideology rooted in "human progress." Adolf Hitler firmly believed that the Aryan race was genetically superior to any other on earth. This idea sprang from Darwin's process of natural selection and was twisted even further by the mind of famed atheist philosopher, Friedrich Nietzsche. The blond-haired, blue-eyed members of the Aryan race were the next step in the evolutionary process. In the fight for the survival of the fittest, Hitler firmly believed the Aryans to be the fittest. And what better way to demonstrate superiority than by subduing the world?[1]

Unlike Nebuchadnezzar, Hitler would never see his vision for the great city realized. The same dream for a city that had lived in the minds of Nimrod, Nebuchadnezzar, and Nero slipped away from Adolf Hitler in suicide. Though Hitler's dream for Berlin died with him, one thing was clear: Satan's desire to establish the great city was alive and well in the twentieth century.

Living in the Prelude to the Great City

Since the height and glory of first-century Rome, Babylon has not found another embodiment. Other empires have risen and fallen, but never has a single city returned to the height and splendor of ancient Rome. Had Adolf Hitler succeeded in his aspirations to develop atomic weapons and dominate the world, it is almost certain that Berlin would have become the new Babylon.

There is an overwhelming sense that we are entering the final generations before the return of Christ. The rebirth of the nation of Israel after nearly 2,000 years of exile is

[1]   To read more about the relationship between Darwin, Nietzsche, and Hitler, see Taha, *Nietzsche, Prophet of Nazism*.

evidence that we are entering the final part of God's plan for this age. There is growing anticipation that an apocalyptic age is approaching. Interest in biblical prophecy is snowballing. Best-selling books and blockbuster movies play on fears that the world is about to come to an end. The earth stands in suspense under an almost universal conviction that a massive global transition is about to occur. Scientists, economists, and politicians are making predictions that could be taken right out of the pages of prophetic Scripture.

What is even more convincing—a sign that Christ's return is approaching—is that international missions organizations report that the gospel will soon reach every corner of the world.[2] Jesus prophesied that once this Great Commission had been fulfilled, the end would come (Mt. 24:14). When we discern the signs of the times, it is undeniable— we are living in the eleventh hour of human history.[3]

According to Bible prophecy, several events must come to pass before Jesus will return. The seventeenth and eighteenth chapters of the book of Revelation declare that the city of Babylon will rise one final time in the days preceding the second coming of Christ. This ancient prophecy tells of Babylon's greatest embodiment.

Many powerful cities exist in the world today. But not a single one of them could be mistaken as the great city the book of Revelation describes. Yet unmistakable signs and trends signify that the atmosphere is astir with an ancient influence. There are clear indications that we are living in

[2] "Absolutely, the Great Commission can be fulfilled in our lifetimes; from the way God is moving today, even without some terrific eye of faith, I have been persuaded it will be fulfilled in our lifetimes and I personally think in the next decade." Douglass, "Endorsements."

[3] In Matthew 16:1–4, Jesus rebukes the Sadducees and Pharisees for their lack of discernment of the current prophetic season.

the twilight of Babylon the Great. Globalization, postmodern culture, and human trafficking are evidence we are entering the beginning phase of Satan's endgame: his final onslaught to pave the way for the Antichrist.

Globalization: The Reversal of Genesis 11

> Clearly . . . it is now possible for more people than ever to collaborate and compete in real time with more other people on more different kinds of work from more different corners of the planet and on a more equal footing than at any previous time in the history of the world . . . We are now connecting all the knowledge centers on the planet together into a single global network, which . . . could usher in an amazing era of prosperity, innovation, and collaboration.[4]
> —Thomas L. Friedman

Before the Tower of Babel was built, the earth spoke only one language. Every member of that community could freely communicate their personal ambitions without hindrance, and the single language greatly expedited their dark efforts to defy God. To stem the tide of this pervading evil, God dispersed the people by confusing their languages.

Common language was the underlying context that accelerated the Babylonians advance into spiritual darkness. It wasn't that language was intrinsically evil. Rather, it merely served to network inherently sinful humans. It is undeniable; fallen humans become far more degenerate together than they do separately. If two darkened minds are worse than one, a unified network of them is catastrophic.

---

[4] Friedman, *The World is Flat*, 8.

What God has separated, humans are once again joining together. Confusing the languages at the Tower of Babel effectively halted the human conspiracy against God. In stark contrast to the effects of Genesis 11, we are seeing the world become a unified global community. Globalization is the irresistible integration of national economies, societies, and cultures.

In our day the confusion of languages is a non-issue. As the Aramaic language united ancient Mesopotamia and the Greek language united the Roman Empire, the earth has been brought together once again by a common language: English. And where English isn't spoken, language barriers are easily overcome through technology.

The primary catalyst for a common language is the growing reality of global commerce. Global commerce is the greatest force at work in uniting the earth today. The world is looking more and more like the Roman Empire, as nation after nation enjoys the benefits of doing business in the global village. The vast wealth and resources of the world are changing hands across international boundaries every day. The burgeoning global network of commercial enterprise is connecting the world in an unmistakable way.

Travel and knowledge have advanced more in the past hundred years than in all of human history prior. World travel is now so prevalent that many people think nothing of traveling to the other side of the earth. Information sharing has reached such historic levels that not only do we regularly converse internationally; we even play video games with one another internationally. Many of the explosive technological advances we have made in recent years were spawned by the advent of the Internet. It has connected the world like no other tool in human history, allowing us to share information globally in real time. Advances in transportation and information technology have made our world smaller and more accessible than ever before.

The foreign policy of the United States has been a key driving force of globalization. The ideologies of freedom and democracy have prevailed in much of the world because of US influence. For years the United States has exerted unparalleled economic and political influence in the nations. US foreign policy has helped to lay the modern-day foundations of the global community.[5]

The Financial Crisis

Recently our increasingly interconnected world has shown vulnerability. When the US economy stumbled, the whole world suffered. International markets around the globe reacted negatively. This volatility proved just how interdependent national economies have become. Now the US financial system is faced with a fundamental dilemma. How long can policies of fiscal irresponsibility be sustained? History has answered that question many times. It is about to be answered again.

As US economic influence wanes, the global community is becoming stronger. Like Dr. Frankenstein, the United States has created a monster that is beyond its control. We can only watch as the monster breaks free from our laboratory and makes his way down the street. The global community that the US has done so much to establish is now taking on a life of its own and turning against its master.

Nothing accelerates change like crisis. Undergoing the greatest economic contraction since the Great Depression

[5]   To read about how American foreign policy has reshaped the global community, see Mead, *Special Providence*.

has opened the door to the unthinkable. The US financial crisis seems to be paving the way for a single global e-currency. The arrival of any such new global economic system will threaten the very fabric of liberty that undergirds the Constitution of the United States. To adopt a global currency is to begin the journey toward unconditional surrender of national sovereignty and the tyranny of the Antichrist that will soon follow.

We are on the brink of the greatest consolidation of economic power in history. The failure of the US financial system is leading to a total restructuring of the global financial system. A world currency, a world central bank, and a world stock market will inevitably follow. Once established, a fully centralized global financial system will almost certainly initiate a cascading effect that will usher in the birth of a new world order.

Hellenism of the Twenty-First Century

For Babylon to arise, the world must be united. We have seen how the world is now interconnected through language, technology, and commerce. But one tie holds the world together with ancient bonds. A dark ideology is rising that has been uniting the world since the Tower of Babel. This ancient lie has been repackaged again and again with devastating effectiveness. Its latest version comes with the label of "postmodernism."

Postmodernism is the Hellenism of the twenty-first century. As Alexander the Great united the world with the culture of Greece, today's world is being united by postmodern culture. Scholars all have differing views of when this trend began. Some argue for the fall of the Berlin Wall, while others point to the "summer of love" in 1967. While the first waves of postmodernism may have washed over America in the late 1960s, the roots of postmodernism reach back to the Tower of Babel.

The postmodern worldview is best understood in relationship to modernism. Modernism is the view that arose from the "modern era," which began in the late nineteenth and early twentieth century. This worldview attempted to define life with systematic and concrete ideas. Modernism sought to understand reality. But now the "modern age" is over. On the heels of the rigid intellectual effort to define and control reality has come a completely different animal: postmodernism.

Postmodernism has successfully seduced the world into embracing the two ideological pillars of Babylon: religious pluralism and moral relativism (a.k.a. idolatry and immorality). Often expressed under the banners of tolerance and diversity, postmodern culture has cut every tie to the social constraints of the past. Morality and spirituality are not grounded in any one set of beliefs. Postmodern spirituality integrates any or all false religious ideas as it pleases the individual, because "all spiritual paths lead to the same god." Whether one believes that everyone is part of God or there is no God at all, all beliefs—no matter how far fetched or contradictory—are ascribed equal validity.

Moral Relativism

> Everyone did what was right in his own eyes.
> —Judges 21:25b

Postmodern morality is founded solely upon the bedrock of individual perspective. No outside authority can dictate what is right and wrong. Any "meta-narrative" is viewed with resentful suspicion as a will to power.[6] Questions of morality are not concerned with ultimate reality. Rather, any moral issue is settled by what seems right to the individual. The postmodern thinks that if one believes that homosexuality is wrong, then that individual shouldn't practice it. But that individual has no right to tell another individual that what they are doing is morally wrong based on convictions formed from an ultimate reality. In postmodernism, all moral beliefs are equally valid and/or equally meaningless. Most in our culture now believe sin has nothing to do with God; sin is merely an individual choice.

The human mind cannot embrace evil ideas and practices without becoming delusional. In rejecting truth, postmodern culture has chosen partnership with the kingdom of darkness, and as a result reason itself is being abandoned. Contradictions and inconsistencies no longer trouble the mind. It doesn't matter what one believes, as long as one is "happy" believing it. Postmodernism has erased right and wrong from western society. The concept of sin is anathema to the postmodern culture, yet sin itself is fully embraced and agreement with darkness is hailed as a triumph of freedom.

The Seduction of False Religion

> Their land is filled with idols; they bow down to the work of their hands, to what their own fingers have made.
> —Isaiah 2:8

The most important issue on the postmodern agenda is "progression." And in the mind of the postmodern person,

---

[6] A meta-narrative is an overarching story that explains the world (for example, the biblical worldview: God created the world, the fall, and redemption).

the greatest threat to human progress is religion. Religious beliefs have divided the world since the beginning of time. But to the postmodern ideology, religions are simply different paths leading to the same spiritual reality. According to postmodern thinking, what is needed for "progress" is for the world to embrace religious pluralism. The call to religious inclusion is the latest appeal to abandon God's Word in order to pursue the "greater good of humanity." It is the very same lie that inspired the Tower of Babel.

Once again we can see Satan working to inspire the human race to unite with the seduction of false religion. Rock stars and charities are calling for interfaith cooperation to "end extreme poverty" because we all serve the same god.[7] Popular talk show hosts are openly endorsing cult leaders, seducing their viewers to abandon the truth for a more "open-minded" approach to spirituality.[8] The World Council of Religious Leaders seeks to identify "universal values" in order to create a lasting world peace.[9]

[7] "The Torah instructs Jews to care for the poor through acts of compassion and loving kindness. In the Gospel of Matthew, Jesus teaches that what is done unto the poor is done unto Him. Zakat, serving the suffering of humanity, is one of the five pillars of Islam. We can all live our beliefs by standing up for those living in extreme poverty." Aaron Banks, "ONE Sabbath: Live Your Beliefs," One.org.

[8] Oprah Winfrey invites her viewers to take online classes that teach the principles of Eckhart Tolle. Tolle writes, "When I occasionally quote the words of Jesus or the Buddha . . . or from other teachings, I do so not in order to compare, but to draw your attention to the fact that in essence there is and always has been only one spiritual teaching, although it comes in many forms." Tolle, *The Power of Now*, 9.

[9] "By promoting the universal human values shared by all religious traditions and by uniting the human community for times of world prayer and meditation, the Council seeks to aid in the development of the inner qualities and external conditions needed for the creation of a more peaceful, just and sustainable world society." World Council of Religious Leaders, "About the World Council of Religious Leaders."

The emphasis on "tolerance" and indifference toward the truth are bringing liberal Jews and Christians together with moderate Muslims to create a world-uniting religion of tolerance and peace. While many see syncretism as the only logical answer to unite the world, God sees something entirely different. He sees a demonic power that can best be described as a prostitute.

The great hypocrisy of the postmodern call to "religious inclusion" and "tolerance for all" is that it does not extend to the Bible. A true postmodern believer must be able to "tolerate" every form of deception, yet firmly oppose the truth. The postmodern condemns faith in the Word of God as exclusive and socially disruptive; conviction about ultimate truth is deemed fallacious, arrogant, and at times a dangerous obstacle to human progress. We are drawing closer to the days when Christians will be labeled "haters of humanity" just as they were in first-century Rome.

The Commercial Sex Industry

> For all nations have fallen by the wine of the passion of her sexual immorality.
> —Revelation 18:3

Previously considered marginal, the sex industry has evolved into one of the most dominant economic forces in the world. Today over one billion people have access to the Internet, and there is no industry as pervasive as Internet pornography. Millions of sites and billions of dollars are devoted to it. Pornography is a thirteen-billion-dollar global business. Every second, $3,075 is being spent on porn, and 28,000 Internet users are viewing it.[10]

The commercial sex industry has awakened an

[10] McDonough-Taub, "Porn at Work."

unprecedented demand for illicit sex. Men are left grop-
ing for the actualization of nefarious sexual fantasies. Ir-
responsible sex is glorified and glamorized. Women are
presented as sexual objects, and men as mindless, sex-
mongering beasts. The world of entertainment has rede-
fined love, beauty, intimacy, and even marriage. The result
is universal sexual hysteria and untold millions who will
pay to feed their appetite. Behind it all is a media machine
driven by corporate greed.

Like first-century Rome, every kind of sexual lust is
embraced and celebrated. The sexual mores that once
governed public life are quickly fading. Fornication is now
the norm in relationships. Homosexuals are demanding
social legitimacy. What was once forbidden by past generations is now openly accepted in our day. The institution
of marriage has been so undermined by the plague of divorce; it is now an afterthought for nearly everyone except
for gay and lesbian activists. And while sexual immorality
is being embraced as a way of life, the porn culture continues to bleed through every form of media and to touch
every public sphere. Billboards, magazines, television, and
popular music all attest to the intoxicating power sexual
immorality has on our culture.

The Rise of Human Trafficking

> And the merchants of the earth weep and mourn
> for her, since no one buys their cargo anymore,
> cargo of gold, silver, jewels . . . and slaves, that
> is, human souls.
>   —Revelation 18:11–13

One of the most shocking and troubling prophecies of
Revelation 18 is that Babylon the Great will be the center of

a global slave trade. It seems unfathomable that the human race is destined to once again descend into the abysmal cesspool of widespread systemic oppression. Previous generations have spiritualized this passage in Revelation, explaining away its explicit implications. How could slavery reemerge in the context of a modern-day civilized society advancing in virtually every realm of human potential? Yet the prophecy is clear. State-sponsored human slavery will return in the end times.

Many are unaware that the shocking reality of human slavery is already upon us. The modern-day slave trade is rapidly cascading into one of the most lucrative commercial enterprises in the world. According to many sources, human trafficking is a thirty-two-billion-dollar per year industry. Women and children are for sale in virtually every corner of the globe. Experts estimate that there are over 27 million slaves on the earth today, which is more than during the height of the transatlantic slave trade.

Human traffickers primarily target young women and children. The defenseless victims are imprisoned, brutalized, and exploited in black-market prostitution rings as veritable sex slaves. The vicious and insatiable lust awakened by the commercial sex industry is creating a demand that traffickers are eager to supply. What we are witnessing is nothing less than the commodification of a generation.

Déjà Vu

The promises of Satan are not new. Through thousands of years, we have seen humans fall to his deceptions. At the Tower of Babel, the people were duped into pursuing their own fame. Nebuchadnezzar led the citizens of Babylon to believe that he was chosen by the gods to build the great city as a physical expression of the spiritual reality of the gods. The Romans thoroughly believed in "eternal Rome." The world's greatest civilizations have been lured time and again with dark promises. It's happening again in our day, and once again the nations are signing on.

From the commercial explosion of the sex industry to the rise of human trafficking, the days we live in are merely the latest expression of an ancient demonic strategy. The financial crisis is opening the door for a fully centralized global economic system that will inevitably undermine national sovereignty and provide the impetus for world government. Postmodernism is the Hellenism of the twenty-first century, uniting world culture. Like the builders of the Tower of Babel, the religious leaders are coming together in the name of human progress. These trends make it clear that we are living in the prelude to Babylon's final embodiment.

THIRTEEN
THE REVOLUTION

Bailout Nation

There was a time in America when people responded to a national crisis by turning to God in prayer—a time when calamity caused us to look inward at our moral failures and upward for divine help. Those days are gone. Now, when natural disasters strike, we expect FEMA to rescue us. When fear of a possible pandemic rises, we expect the CDC to have a vaccine at the ready. This growing expectation is escalating so outrageously that we even expect our national treasury to bail out financial institutions whose reckless business practices brought on insolvency. As our nation departs from the principles that made it great, more and more we look to government as our god.

Like the prodigal son awaking to find he had wasted his entire inheritance on riotous living, America is awaking to a whole a new reality. The party is drawing to a close and as we slowly sober up, we can see famine looming on the horizon. The only question that remains to be answered is, will America finally turn back to God in her trouble, or will she continue to seek another solution? The soul of our nation hangs in the balance.

But this isn't just a problem for America. The entire world is being faced with a cosmic dilemma. The Bible teaches that God sends trouble to nations so that they will turn to Him. Faltering economies, terror attacks, and natural disasters are all messages from a loving God who wants to save us from ourselves. But when the nations raise a rebellious fist to God in the time of trouble and turn to government as the solution, Satan has sprung his trap. Power-hungry government officials are glad to step in and fill the void. This is the path to the loss of every freedom— a path that leads directly through the gates of Babylon.

The Church today is almost completely unaware of what is at stake. As many of the Jewish people lost sight of who they were in the Babylonian captivity, countless saints today are losing sight of eternity. While in exile, many of the captive Jews began to esteem their homes and businesses above their calling as God's chosen, losing sight of what made them distinct. That same blindness is settling into the Church. An overwhelming sense of aimlessness and confusion is fogging the Church's sense of destiny and purpose.

Many have abandoned what God has placed in their hearts because everything in their circumstances seems to contradict His promises. God has spoken to numerous individuals about what He is going to do in the coming days. He has promised to release His presence and power like never before in history. Yet we have seen the exact opposite. Everywhere we turn, there is compromise and lukewarm affections for God. Instead of seeing the power of God manifested, we have seen the undisturbed pursuit of wealth and easy living. That is about to change.

The Zeal of the Lord

Immense revolution is right around the corner. The way that Christianity is expressed in the earth will undergo radical transformation. The current mindset and lifestyle of western Christianity will not survive the coming crisis.

The biggest problem facing the Church isn't economic collapse, national calamity, or treacherous policy makers of a godless government. The biggest problem isn't even Satan's murderous rage. Our biggest problem is that we serve a God who will stop at nothing to possess whole-hearted worshipers. He will not leave us alone in our spiritual compromise. This is the God of Jeremiah the prophet, who used the pagan king Nebuchadnezzar to refine His people; He is the same Jesus who overturned tables in the temple. The true source of the coming trouble is a God who cannot stand the sight of compromise and will go to any extreme to drive it out.

The days that precede Jesus' return will be the most terrible and glorious in history. Everything in the earth, sky, and sea will be shaken.[1] The greatest of evils will be unleashed in the earth—wars, disease, famine, and natural disasters (Mt. 24:7–8). Human history will reach its climax as the earth groans under the full weight of God's wrath and the unbridled rage of Satan (Rev. 12:12). Many will be paralyzed with fear in the face of the coming storm (Lk. 21:26).

Though the coming days will be fearful, they will also be the most glorious days for the Church. As the first generations of Christians were empowered to overcome Rome and Nero, the last generations will be empowered to overcome Babylon the Great and the Antichrist. In the

---

[1] The seal/trumpet/bowl judgment series described in Revelation emphasizes that every realm of the created order will be touched by God's wrath. See especially Revelation 10:5–7.

darkness and oppression of this end-time confrontation will come the Church's finest hour. God will purify and ready the Bride for the coming of His Son.

This begs the question: how will we get there from where we are today? By all appearances, it seems like the Church is far from being ready for the incredible magnitude of the approaching trouble. But God has a plan to change everything in a moment.

Fire from the Altar

In the book of Revelation, the apostle John enters God's throne room and is given a behind-the-scenes look at the role of the Church in the end times. God invites John into the governmental center of the universe to see events that will have global implications in the final days of history.

> And another angel came and stood at the altar with a golden censer, and he was given much incense to offer with the prayers of all the saints on the golden altar before the throne, and the smoke of the incense, with the prayers of the saints, rose before God from the hand of the angel. Then the angel took the censer and filled it with fire from the altar and threw it on the earth.
> —Revelation 8:3–5

In this stunning prophetic revelation, John watches God's end-time drama unfold before his eyes. John sees seven angels with trumpets standing before God. These are the seven trumpets that are about to release unthinkable calamities into the earth (Rev. 8–9). In the prelude to the blowing of the trumpets, John sees another angel approach the altar with a golden censer. From that golden censer, the smoke of incense is billowing as an offering to God. Among the incense are the prayers of all the saints. Once the incense of the saints arises before God, the angel takes the golden censer and fills it with fire from the altar. He then throws that fire onto the earth.

This heavenly fire has two dramatic dimensions. The first dimension of God's fire is incineration. When God releases this fire, it will have devastating consequences for those who have joined Satan's rebellion. This fire will mark the beginning of God's end-time judgments. These judgments are sent to cut down everything that stands against the kingdom of God and the return of Jesus Christ to the earth.

The second dimension of God's fire is empowerment. God has a plan to empower His people to stand against overwhelming odds. The Church will once again operate in the power she had in the first century, and in even greater levels of power. The "greater works" that Jesus promised His disciples will be operative in the final days of this age (6 Jn. 14:12; Joel 2:28–32). Supernatural power to preach, heal, drive out demons, and even raise the dead will be activated in God's final campaign to glorify His Son in a fallen world.

The Global Prayer Movement

God will not send holy fire to empower the Church until there is a unified global cry for it. Since the beginning of time, God has demonstrated kingdom power through the ministry of intercession. The magnitude of what He has promised to do in the end times will only come in response to worldwide prayer.

One of the most telling signs that we are approaching the end of the age is that God is raising up a global prayer movement. Around the world, God is restoring the foundations of prayer. In cities throughout the entire earth, God is raising up prayer rooms full of people who will continue to intercede day and night until Jesus returns. It is happening in our time.

To understand why a global prayer movement is a critical aspect of God's end-time plan, we must return to the book of Revelation. Before God's judgment series begins, John sees twenty-four elders falling down before the Lamb of God. In the hands of each of these elders are two things—a harp in one hand, a golden bowl in the other. John sees that the golden bowls have become full with incense. This is the same incense that the angel offered to God; it is the prayers of the saints (Rev. 5:8). Before God begins to judge the earth and empower the Church to usher in the return of His Son, the golden bowls must become full with prayer.

Just like Noah's sacrifice was a sweet-smelling aroma to the Lord, so the growing fervency and unity of the Church in prayer will one day crescendo into a global symphony that ultimately invokes the manifest presence and power of God. This concert of prayer is instrumental in releasing the fire of God upon the earth. The Church will enter into her finest hour as she joins with the cry of the apostle John for Jesus to "come quickly" (Rev. 22:17).

Ancient Opposition

> If they have called the master of the house Beelzebub, how much more will they malign those of his household?
>
> —Matthew 10:25b

Along with the rise of a global prayer movement have come the first chilling winds of religious persecution in

America. Terms like "radical clerics," "religious extremists," and "domestic terrorists" are not just for Al-Qaeda anymore. Now they apply to religious conservatives who oppose abortion.[2] For over two centuries now, we have lived without the scourge of state-sponsored religious persecution. But the winds of change are beginning to blow in America.

The rising tide of persecution means we are in good company (Mt. 5:11–12). John the Baptist spent years in the desert. He didn't fit into the religious system. He was an outsider, a stranger. John the Baptist spurned the glory and power of Rome. While the chief priests and scribes were wearing glorious apparel, John was wrapped in a camel's skin. While the political leaders in Israel were feasting on every delicacy, John ate bugs and raided beehives. He and his disciples were known for the intensity with which they held to fasting (Mt. 9:14). For his uncompromising devotion to God, the religious leaders of his day said he was demonized (Mt. 11:18).

The same things that made John the Baptist a stranger in his day are going to make us strangers in ours. For instance, in America the threat of "hate legislation" continues to eat away basic freedoms of the First Amendment, making it a crime to stand against sin. Publicly opposing abortion or homosexual marriage is labeled dangerous extremism. Jesus warned that devotion to God would be

[2] "If you're an anti-abortion activist, or if you display political paraphernalia supporting a third-party candidate or a certain Republican member of Congress, if you possess subversive literature, you very well might be a member of a domestic paramilitary group. That's according to 'The Modern Militia Movement,' a report by the Missouri Information Analysis Center (MIAC), a government collective that identifies the warning signs of potential domestic terrorists for law enforcement communities." Miller, "Fusion Centers Expand Criteria to Identify Militia Members."

demonized by the world. The sobering reality is that what we are seeing today is merely the beginning of this trend. The intensity of Christian persecution in the end times will surpass even that of ancient Rome.[3]

The Road Map

Understanding Babylon is the key to discerning the current prophetic season. It is imperative that we find ourselves in history. If we cannot identify where we are in God's prophetic calendar, the events that lie ahead will ambush us, bringing unnecessary fear and confusion. If we don't know where we are and what time it is, we will be imprisoned in the confusion of the coming crisis.

As Babylon rises toward her ultimate expression, the earth is under transition. Behind the curtain of the unseen, a familiar force is at work. Satan is again working to unify the earth in sinful defiance of God. The current rise of postmodernism, sexual immorality, and false religion attests that Babylon is in the prelude to her final and greatest manifestation.

We know how Daniel lived a focused life while in Nebuchadnezzar's court. We also know that the first-century church did not compromise under Rome's threats and temptations. Now it's our turn. We must do what they did. God has promised to send holy fire to empower His Church to withstand the onslaught and accomplish His end-time plan—to provoke the nation of Israel to jealousy and usher in the return of Christ.

---

[3] "And I saw the woman, drunk with the blood of the saints" (Rev. 17:6).

PART V
BABYLON THE GREAT

FOURTEEN
THE GREAT HARLOT

THE ORIGINAL SETTING FOR GOD'S COMMUNION with man was the garden of Eden. When Jesus returns and creation is restored, the place of communion will not be a garden; it will be a city. Before the foundations of the earth were laid, God ordained that He would dwell with His people in an eternal city called the New Jerusalem. This city will not arise by human effort, nor will it come from the earth; it will come down from God out of heaven (Rev. 21:2). Though we cannot see it now, Jesus promised He was ascending to heaven to prepare a place for His own (Jn. 14:2). Abraham was looking forward to this city (Heb. 11:10). Adorned with unthinkable glory, the New Jerusalem is not merely the divine material and architecture of which it is constructed; it is the community of the redeemed. In other words, this city isn't just bricks and buildings; the city is a Bride. It is the place of God's restored communion with mankind through the Lord Jesus. It will be within this city that:

> The dwelling place of God [will be] with man. He
> will dwell with them, and they will be His people,

and God Himself will be with them as their God. He will wipe away every tear from their eyes, and death shall be no more, neither shall there be mourning nor crying nor pain anymore, for the former things have passed away.

—Revelation 21:3–4

The Demonic New Jerusalem

Before God rejoins heaven and earth, forever healing the created realm, Satan will be allowed to make one last attempt to bring the full power of hell into the earth. God is not the only one with a plan to make a dwelling place with men. Two opposing forces are working to bring the earth into subjection. What began at Babel through Nimrod will be finished through the eschatological Antichrist. Satan will make one last attempt to gather the nations in unified defiance against God, a final campaign to bring fallen humans into full agreement with the kingdom of darkness.

Satan has been actively working to recover what he lost when he led the failed rebellion against God. Though banished from its glory forever, the devil still remembers what heaven is like. Satan was intimately acquainted with the celestial city; he worshiped at the very throne of God. He felt the awe of being part of an innumerable army of angels fully engaged in abandoned worship. He remembers the unbroken adoration and the unspeakable refulgence of the glory of God. Every moment, he is haunted by his memory and consumed by the lust to rule and be worshiped as God. And we are now in the final years of the devil focusing every effort to recreate the darkest imaginable version of the heavenly city, the city he once experienced as an archangel.

For the full fury of hell to be released into the earth,

human sin must prepare the way. Satan will not be able to usurp the level of authority he needs without first being given it freely by human agreement. To garner this level of authority over fallen men, Satan will incorporate an ancient strategy. He will inspire the building of a city that will lead the world into his power. Satan's last attempt will be to win the hearts of fallen humans through the promise of a golden civilization, the greatest city in the history of the world. It will be through the global influence of this final city that the earth will be united and prepared to worship him.

Something about a city excites and seduces the sinful hearts of men. The grand buildings of magnificent architecture inspire pride in human accomplishment. The promise of profit lures money-loving merchants. Men and women flock to the city in pursuit of fame. Politicians lust after the unparalleled opportunity for power that the masses afford. And the excitement of immoral pleasures drives the godless to gather at the hot spots of its nightlife. The greatest city in all history would be an almost perfect trap with which to snare the world and fill it with sin.

Nimrod dreamed of a mighty city when he led the builders of Babel. Nebuchadnezzar, the Great Builder, spent his life in pursuit of creating a city that mirrored the home of the gods. Nero set Rome ablaze in hopes that a golden city would be rebuilt in its place. Adolf Hitler worked fervently with his chief architect, Albert Speer, to make Berlin the greatest capital in the world. These dark dreams for an eternal city that have dominated the imaginations of evil men speak of the purpose still alive in Satan's mind today.

The power that united human civilization in defiance of God to build the Tower of Babel will reach its culmination in the years ahead. A city will soon arise that far surpasses the power and influence of first-century Rome. It will be the political, economic, and cultural capital of the world. A deceptive ideology exalting human progress will intoxicate the world, as this city becomes the center for every form of immoral and idolatrous practice. From this place, a network of false religion will be born that will ensnare the entire world.

Babylon Unleashed

During all of human history, God's sovereign hand has restrained the spirit of Babylon from being fully released. Historically, when the harlot has taken her throne in the lead city of the earth, God has held her back from fully opening the gateway of the gods. He confused language in Babel. He held the megalomaniac Nebuchadnezzar in check. Not even the harlot's manifestation through mighty Rome was ever permitted to fully actualize. Time and again, the demonic agenda to release the full measure of Satan's rage through Babylon has been restrained by God. But the day is coming when God will not restrain the full influence of the harlot spirit for a season.

Thousands of years ago, Zechariah was given insight into the spiritual reality behind Babylon. Standing face to face with an angel, the prophet was shown this mystery in a vision. Zechariah saw a basket with a cover of lead weight being sent out into the earth. The angel explained that within it were contained the sins of all the land. The angel then opened the basket to show Zechariah what was inside.

> And behold, the leaden cover was lifted, and there was a woman sitting in the basket! And

he said, "This is Wickedness." And he thrust her back into the basket, and thrust down the leaden weight on its opening. Then I lifted my eyes and saw, and behold, two women coming forward! The wind was in their wings. They had wings like the wings of a stork, and they lifted up the basket between earth and heaven. Then I said to the angel who talked with me, "Where are they taking the basket?" He said to me, "To the land of Shinar, to build a house for it. And when this is prepared, they will set the basket down there on its base."

—Zechariah 5:7–11

Two familiar features stand out in this vision: the contents in the basket and its destination place. Within the basket is a woman whom the angel identifies with the adjective "Wickedness." Could this be the same woman that John sees in his vision on the Isle of Patmos, whose title contains "Mother of Prostitutes and Abominations of the Earth"? This question is answered affirmatively when we consider the land for which the basket is destined: the land of Shinar. The cryptic reference to the land of Shinar immediately draws the reader's attention to the Genesis 11 narrative, where the first expression of the harlot spirit invaded human history. In this vision, Zechariah sees the very same harlot spirit that John would see more fully nearly 600 years later. The woman in the basket destined for the land of Shinar is none other than the demonic principality at work behind Babylon.

The other features in Zechariah's vision are not as familiar to us, but after considering the text they become clearer. The two women with storks' wings who carry the basket have two mandates: to transport the basket by air to the land of Shinar, and to build a house for it.

While the exact nature and timing of their assignment isn't clear, some general observations can be made. The first is that, though the harlot spirit is contained within the basket, her influence is not entirely restrained. The idea of atmospheric influence with demonic spiritual power is clearly stressed in this vision. The first indication is the phrase that the angel speaks to Zechariah when he says, "this is the basket that is going out" (Zech. 5:6). The operative words in this phrase are "going out." From Zechariah's previous vision, we know that this phrase is meant to imply widespread influence.[1]

The influence of the woman who is going out into the earth is also clearly implied in this vision by the spiritual language Zechariah used. The women with wings like a stork are said to have "wind in their wings" and they lift up the basket "between heaven and earth." These two aspects stress that spiritual activity is at work empowering this transaction. And we can be sure that this spiritual influence is demonic because the women have wings like a stork. The very fact that women have wings like that of a bird that God declared unclean clearly demonstrates that the spiritual power he saw in the vision was evil.[2]

Zechariah is told that the women will carry the basket until they build a house for it in the land of Shinar. Once these two evil spirits carry the basket out into all the earth,

[1] In the previous vision, Zechariah tells of a scroll that "goes out over the face of the whole land" (5:3). These are the very same words the angel used to describe the influence of the basket in verse 5. Clearly this expression is meant to denote widespread influence.

[2] Lev. 11:19. It is highly unlikely that the Jewish prophet would use an unclean bird as a metaphor to symbolize a holy action on behalf of God.

spreading its influence and building it a house, the basket will be set down upon the earth. At that time, the earth will experience the harlot unleashed. Zechariah was shown a stunning picture of the harlot spirit of Babylon in the end times. Its influence would be spread throughout the earth as the nations gather together. But the harlot power will not be fully released until the great city is built.

FIFTEEN

UNVEILING THE GREAT HARLOT

WHILE EXILED ON THE ISLE OF PATMOS, John the apostle was given a divine revelation of the days in which Jesus would return to earth. In this vision John saw the culmination of human history. He saw the days when sin would be fully expressed, the fury of Satan's rage would be unleashed, and God's wrath would be poured out in full measure. Amazingly, the apostle John was looking ahead nearly 2,000 years to see the events that would happen on earth in the generation of the Lord's return.

John sees the final crescendo of human history, the days when the ancient power of Babylon will have its fullest manifestation. The prophet Zechariah saw a woman contained in a basket; John sees her set free. Zechariah saw the prelude to the great city. John sees the great city fully operational. What was conceived in the city of Babel, continued by the Babylonians, and revived by Rome will have its ultimate expression in the darkest city in history. The budding expressions of earlier versions of Babylon become fully developed in Babylon the Great. The fullest and clearest portrait of Babylon the Great comes to us in the final chapters of the book of Revelation.

> Then one of the seven angels who had the seven bowls came and said to me, ""Come, I will show you the judgment of the great prostitute who is seated on many waters."
>
> —Revelation 17:1

> And the woman that you saw is the great city that has dominion over the kings of the earth.
>
> —Revelation 17:18

One of the angels with the final bowls of judgment tells John that he will see the day of God's wrath on the great prostitute. The angel takes John on a journey to show him the greatest city in the history of the world. But John does not see the city's rise nor does he see it in the zenith of its power; rather, he witnesses the final hours of the city's great fall. As a prophetic onlooker to the judgment of the prostitute, John records two polar opposite responses to Babylon's fall. He records the response of a rejoicing host in heaven as judgment is meted out, and the response of shocked humans on earth reeling at the sight of their great city being crushed.

Who Is the Great Harlot?

There are many theories about what Babylon could be. But John is told explicitly that the woman he sees seated upon many waters is the great city. While this may be a simple and straightforward statement, it goes a long way to eliminate what Babylon is not. The great harlot is not a country or a nation.[1] Babylon is not two or more cities.[2] The

---

[1]   Therefore Babylon cannot be the United States of America.

[2]   This is contrary to the idea that Babylon the Great will consist of a

prostitute is not merely an economic system.[3] Nor is the prostitute merely a certain category of false religion.[4] Each of these facets are necessary to understanding the nature and character of Babylon, but the angel tells John quite plainly that the great prostitute is a city.

While it is true that, before anything else, Babylon the Great is an actual city, it is also clear that behind the city there is a specific power at work. The city has a persona; its persona is that of a harlot. A personal force at work behind the scene deceives men and infuses the great city with the personality of a seductress. This is a spiritual power that has led human civilization in defiance of God at different times since the flood. To understand the Babylon phenomenon, we must recognize that an ancient demonic principality is at work behind the great city. Babylon the Great isn't merely the result of repeated human folly best described as harlotry by apocalyptic writers; the dark spiritual reality behind Babylon is a demonic principality working to bring humans in league with the kingdom of darkness.

A City-Centered Empire

> And he carried me away in the Spirit into a wilderness, and I saw a woman sitting on a scarlet beast that was full of blasphemous names, and it had seven heads and ten horns.
> —Revelation 17:3

> And the ten horns that you saw are ten kings.
> —Revelation 17:12

number of cities.

3   Therefore Babylon cannot be capitalism.
4   Therefore Babylon cannot be Catholicism.

3333a

Before John gets to see the judgment of the great prostitute, he is carried away into the desert, where he is privy to a peculiar sight: the harlot riding upon a beast of seven heads and ten horns.[5] This odd vision gives us some idea of how Babylon the Great comes to dominate the earth in the end times. The ten horns that the angel identifies as ten kings indicate that the beast upon which the prostitute rides is not a person but an empire. This is the same beast-empire that the prophet Daniel saw nearly 700 years before (Dan. 7:7–8, 19–25).

This scarlet beast or sinful empire that is prophesied to come in the end times will arise with ten kings or primary political leaders. The harlot riding on the back of this empire is a clear depiction of Babylon the Great as the economic and political capital of the end-time empire. Just as Rome was the center of the Roman Empire and the Babylonian Empire was based in the city of Babylon, so the end-time empire will have its main power base in a single city. It will be a city-centered empire. Babylon the Great will be the primary governmental city, empowered and endorsed by all the kings and the nations of the final empire.

> The waters that you saw, where the prostitute is seated, are the peoples and multitudes and nations and languages.
>
> —Revelation 17:15

[5] Understanding the exact dynamics of the end-time empire from this vision is very difficult. The seven heads of the beast are identified as seven mountains and seven kings (Rev. 17:9–10). There is little agreement among commentators as to what the seven heads of the beast may mean. Some commentators insist that the seven mountains are the seven hills that Rome was known for and the kings are the emperors of Rome. Others understand the seven mountains as the seven empires that had a historical relationship to the nation of Israel (Egypt, Assyria, Babylon, Persia, Greece, Rome, and the Antichrist's empire).

As the economic capital of the end-time empire, Babylon the Great will be, by default, the capital city of the world. The angel interprets the vision John saw and explains that the great city will exercise full political authority over the nations of the earth. The dispersion that God caused at the Tower of Babel will be fully reversed as Babylon the Great brings all the nations and languages of the earth together under her political authority. All will live in the shadow of the authority of Babylon the Great. Just as the decisions made by emperors, senators, and generals in the city of Rome had direct consequences for cities and citizens throughout the entire Roman Empire, so the nations of the earth will be subject to the political decisions that are made in Babylon the Great. The prostitute seated upon many waters and dressed in regal attire demonstrates that the harlot city will bring the earth together and dominate the political landscape in the end times.

The Golden City

> The woman was arrayed in purple and scarlet, and adorned with gold and jewels and pearls, holding in her hand a golden cup full of abominations and the impurities of her sexual immorality. And on her forehead was written a name of mystery: "Babylon the Great, mother of prostitutes and of earth's abominations."
>
> —Revelation 17:4–5

The angel shows John the most garish and tawdry woman imaginable. Decked from head to toe in the most lavish apparel, the harlot city will give new meaning to the excessive lifestyle. Her jewels and garments clearly indicate that Babylon the Great will adorn herself with the vast wealth of the world. The greatest treasures of the nations will pour into the great city. Babylon's museums and galleries will host the most spectacular items. The city's cutting-edge architecture will stun the eye and fascinate the heart. The greatest buildings in history will be erected as advances in architecture reach historic levels. Nero's dream for a city of gold will finally be actualized. Babylon the Great will become the wealthiest city in history as Satan is driven by his own vision of the Celestial City.

The primary reason the wealth of the nations will be concentrated in the city is because Babylon the Great will be the center of the greatest global network of economies in human history.[6] The current combined economic power of New York, Tokyo, and London will pale in comparison to the economic power that will belong to Babylon the Great in the coming days. The city will be the center of a network that will connect the international markets of the world like never before. Technological advances and innovations in global currency will make joining Babylon's network inescapable for all nations. All the merchants of earth will clamor for the opportunity of doing business with Babylon and becoming rich by supplying the city's excesses.

As Babylon the Great overflows with affluence, every imaginable luxury and recreation known to man will be fully indulged in.[7] The best food and drink will be found there, along with the newest technologies, making life as sumptuous as can be imagined. Leisure and recreation will find new summits in Babylon. Its magnificent auditoriums

---

[6] "Adorned with gold, with jewels, and with pearls!" (Rev. 18:11–17).

[7] "The power of her luxurious living . . . she glorified herself and lived in luxury . . . all your delicacies and your splendors are lost to you" (Rev. 18:3, 7, 14).

will play host to the most popular musicians,[8] whose lyrics will endorse the demonic values of the city and play a significant role in advancing Babylon's ideological unity. Babylon's chief priority will be indulging the senses.

The Final Rebellion

The defiant pride that was expressed in seed-form at the Tower of Babel will be fully manifested in Babylon the Great.[9] The ideology of the city will drive fallen humans to pursue "progress" and "achievement" while abandoning all true knowledge of God. The pomp and pride of the city will openly defy the God of the Bible. The citizens will think that they are the crowning achievement of all human history. Babylon the Great will be a city that is undergirded by a blasphemous ideology inspired by the harlot spirit. The lyrics of the songs, the propaganda in the media, the daily headlines, and humanistic slogans will all affirm the antichrist values and beliefs of the great city.

Every culture and society on earth will be deeply affected by the influence of this one city. The world will become a unified network of cities and cultures subject to the political authority of Babylon the Great. The cultures of the world will not only be affected in the more innocuous arenas of fashion trends and business transactions. They will be poisoned at a much more sinister level, influenced to embrace lifestyles of moral decadence and spiritual idolatry. Babylon's worldwide network will not be confined to economics and culture; it will convey a system of belief about morality and spirituality. The entire earth will be corrupted by the

---

[8] "The sound of harpists and musicians, of flute players and trumpeters" (Rev. 18:22).

[9] "As she glorified herself . . . since in her heart she says 'I sit as a queen'" (Rev. 18:7).

sinful influence of the great city.

A unified globe will participate in the immorality of the harlot spirit as her power is fully released in the earth. Nations will be overtaken in the flood of demonic power that will originate in Babylon the Great. The entire earth will be saturated with the practice of sexual immorality.[10] The power emanating from Babylon, seducing the nations to partake in sexual immorality, will be a toxic wine that overcomes all who drink of it. Those who do not resist it will be washed away with it. The harlot spirit will once and for all dupe fallen humans into breaking from traditional moral values. The nations will embrace the false idea that freedom from all sense of morality is the next step in human evolution. The mighty city will be filled with the most perverted of human sexual behaviors and export her lewd practices around the world.

The Worldwide Network of False Religion

Beneath the pervasive influence of sexual immorality in Babylon the Great will be a far darker power. The great city will lead the world in the most abominable spiritual practices. The debauchery of Babylon will, at its idolatrous core, be conjoined with demon worship. Babylon's embrace of syncretism and the worship of all gods will be nothing less than the worship of demons. The true power source of Babylon will be her idolatrous worship. Below the diaphanous surface of fashion and wealth will lie an underbelly of demonic power like the earth has never seen. Though the veneer of Babylon will exalt "the good of humanity," the underlying power that drives the global influence of the city will not be human in origin; it will be satanic.

---

[10] "For all the nations have drunk the wine of the passion of her sexual immorality" (Rev. 18:3).

Human agreement with the kingdom of darkness will lead to an infestation of demon spirits. The sins of Babylon will afford demonic power such a gateway into human affairs as has not been opened since before the flood.[11] Babylon the Great will corrupt the earth and spawn an atmosphere so charged with immorality that the kingdom of darkness will gain free reign. The citizens of Babylon will be helpless against the onslaught of demonic power that they have willingly invited to dominate them.

The greatest evil that Babylon will unleash is the idolatrous network of false religion with which she will ensnare the world. Babylon will bring the nations together by uniting all the world religions into one amalgamation of false spirituality. Just as first-century Rome endorsed a diversity of pagan beliefs, the sorcery of Babylon the Great will exalt the tolerance of nearly all religious beliefs and practices. It will create an idolatrous network of temples that will touch every major city in the world. The false religion of Babylon will see the only hope of humanity residing in the coalescence of all religious belief. The nations will embrace this false religion of Babylon.[12]

The false religion of Babylon the Great will not allow for exclusive spirituality. The harlot religion will teach that Jesus is only one among the many ways into authentic spirituality. Buddhism, Hinduism, Islam, and Judaism will

---

[11] "She has become a dwelling place for demons, a haunt for every unclean spirit, a haunt for every unclean bird . . . and detestable beast" (Rev. 18:2). This passage does not depict a city being forsaken and becoming a wilderness inhabited by wild animals, as was the case for Jeremiah's prophecy of the ancient city of Babylon (Jer. 51:37). The "unclean birds" and "detestable beasts" that the angel speaks of are demonic spirits. See Walvoord, *The Revelation of Jesus Christ,* 259.

[12] "For as were the days of Noah, so will be the coming of the Son of Man" (Mt. 24:37).

be endorsed as equally valid religious beliefs. The harlot religion will denounce the exclusive (yet vital) doctrines of Christianity. All who embrace the harlot religion must reject the Lord Jesus as being the only way to the Father.

The Great Apostasy

The most grievous facet of this worldwide network of false religion is that it will deceive many who consider themselves Christians. Many leaders in the Church will endorse the false religion of Babylon. Both the Lord Jesus and the apostle Paul refer to a period of time when a great number of people will fall away from the Christian faith (Mt. 24:10; 2 Thes. 2:3). The power behind the harlot religion will be so strong and the advantages of compromising with Babylon will be so profitable that many who profess to be Christians will openly endorse and gladly teach the demonic doctrines of Babylon. Just as the chief priests, scribes, and Pharisees were employed and empowered by Rome, leaders in the Church will become puppets of the great harlot. They will lead the way into the great apostasy.

The great apostasy will reveal the true Christians from the false. As the Babylonian captivity sifted the faithful from the unfaithful and as first-century Rome controlled the religious leadership in Jerusalem, Babylon the Great will cause the greatest sifting in Church history. The pressures of the coming religious delusion will reveal who truly belongs to Christ.

As the religious aspect of Babylon grows in global influence, it will ultimately lead to the persecution of the faithful. Though the endorsed religion of Babylon will claim to tolerate all beliefs equally, any "extreme religious beliefs" will be strictly condemned as detrimental to human progress. Nothing will be so vehemently despised in Babylon

as true Christianity. Just as Rome tagged the first genera-
tion of Christians "haters of humanity," the final generation of
Christians will face similar rhetoric and even greater persecu-
tion. In the spirit of John the Baptist, great men and women
of God will stand up against the sorcery and immorality of
Babylon the Great, calling the nations to repent. And just like
John, many of these faithful servants will pay with their lives.
This persecution will become so violent that Babylon the
Great is said to become "drunk" with the blood of martyrs
(Rev. 17:6).

Babylon the Great will be the economic and political
capital of the world. From her high position of authority,
the harlot principality will intoxicate the entire earth with
her teachings and practices. The kingdom of darkness will
seduce the nations into agreement with an evil agenda.
As human sin reaches new levels through idolatry and immorality, demonic power will flood into the earth. Through
Babylon the Great, the gateway of the gods will be opened.
The nations will defy God as they fall for the ancient promise of a "golden civilization" that offers the last hope for
humanity. Behind the scenes, Satan will be working to
condition human hearts for his leadership. Once the inhabitants of the earth become drunk with the wine of Babylon,
Satan's final agenda will be implemented: the Antichrist
will be revealed.

The Rise of the Antichrist

The grip of the harlot principality on the nations will
not last forever. The harlot power will be betrayed, overcome, and stripped of her influence before the city's ultimate judgment comes at the hand of God. This should
be a familiar storyline to us now. We have seen it repeated
over and over again: the people of the earth join together

to build a city in defiance of God, unified in false religion, commerce, and immorality. This city becomes the imperial center of an economic and religious network that corrupts the world with evil beliefs and practices. A figure who appears to be the great hope of the future arises as the primary political leader of that city-based empire. That leader then dissolves the tolerant practices and policies of the city, creating a strict autocracy. Consumed with a satanic lust for power, that leader ultimately declares himself to be a deity and demands worship. It happened in part with Nimrod and Babel. It happened in part with Nebuchadnezzar and Babylon. It happened in part with Nero and Rome. These historical examples foreshadow what is prophesied to happen fully in the end times with the Antichrist and Babylon the Great.

Since the flood, human leaders of vast lands and countries have been hell-bent on demonic agendas. Many tyrants have arisen with Antichrist-like characteristics. History's most extensive prototype of the Antichrist may be the Seleucid tyrant, Antiochus Epiphanes. But Satan has also filled the hearts of several of the Caesars of Rome, not the least of them Nero. In more recent times, Adolf Hitler was consumed with a demonic vision of a Third Reich. Hitler was convinced that Germans would rule a Jew-free world in a thousand-year Nazi reign. Even the leadership of North Korea and Iran in the early twenty-first century continues to be dominated by demonic designs. But all of these examples are only small foreshadowings of the global empire that will arise in the final days of this age, when Satan himself will give his full power to a single human being: the Antichrist.

The Bible prophesies that this man will arise in the end times. Unmatched political genius and military prowess will identify him as a rising star on the world scene. He will broker a historic peace treaty (Dan. 9:27). He will lend his support and openly endorse the new hope that the city and ideology of Babylon the Great promises. He will seem to be Babylon's best advocate. But when the opportune moment comes, he will make the greatest power grab in history and become its fiercest tyrant.

> And the ten horns that you saw are ten kings who have not yet received royal power, but they are to receive authority as kings for one hour, together with the beast. These are of one mind, and they hand over their power and authority to the beast.
>
> —Revelation 17:12–13

The ten kings that head the end-time empire will willingly hand over their royal power to the most evil man in history. It is difficult to deduce what events will lead to this transfer of power. We can only surmise from history and from what we know of the nature of the Antichrist that he will beguile the ten kings with false promises. We know that the Antichrist will deceive with nearly irresistible power (Rev. 13:14). The imperial politics of Babylon the Great could conceivably become so bogged down in bureaucracy that political decision-making will come to a standstill. Will the Antichrist persuade the ten kings that the only way forward will be handing him executive powers? The fact is that the actual political events that lead to this historic transfer of power are cloaked from us for now.[13] But Scripture makes it clear that one way or another the Antichrist will become emperor of the end-time empire.

[13] The prophet Daniel seems to shed some light on this mysterious event (Dan. 7:24).

The Reign of Terror

> And the ten horns that you saw, they and the
> beast will hate the prostitute. They will make
> her desolate and naked, and devour her flesh
> and burn her with fire, for God has put it in their
> hearts to carry out His purpose by being of one
> mind and handing over their royal power to the
> beast, until the words of God are fulfilled.
>
> —Revelation 17:16–17

As the new emperor, the Antichrist will command the military forces of the empire to march against the city of Babylon, introducing his reign of terror with an iron fist. The prominence of the harlot city will be eclipsed by the Antichrist, and Babylon will finally have her true king. As the perverted counterfeit of the New Jerusalem, the harlot city will have prepared herself for her lord. The Antichrist will come to his harlot for the sole purpose of exploiting her global network of economies and temples. Just as Nero set Rome ablaze, the Antichrist will lead the world empire to burn the great city and sweep away all of her religious tolerance and moral freedoms.

Once Babylon is subdued by his power, the Antichrist will implement the fiercest tyranny the world has ever witnessed. He will launch a military campaign against the nation of Israel and execute a plan to systematically exterminate the Jewish people. The tolerant practices of Babylon the Great will be replaced by emperor worship, implemented with legislation, and enforced with capital punishment.[14] The Antichrist will commandeer the economic system of Babylon and institute a global currency that will

---

[14] Rev. 13:15–16.

require a mark. No one will be allowed to participate in commerce without it.

The Mark of the Beast

Idolatry has taken on numerous forms throughout history. But in the final generation of this age, the ultimate idol will be a human being. The Antichrist will exalt himself against all gods and demand to be worshiped as God.[15] During the last hours of human history, no other religion will be tolerated. Ruler worship will be the only legal religious practice and no one will be excused from it. The syncretistic tolerance of Babylon will suddenly be swallowed by the tyrannical intolerance of the Antichrist, as the king of Babylon comes to exploit his harlot. All who take the mark will be required to worship him exclusively. Those who willingly worship the Antichrist will be making their final statement of approval for Satan's leadership in their eternal rejection of the Lord.

> And the dwellers on earth whose names have not been written in the book of life from the foundation of the world will marvel to see the beast . . .
>
> —Revelation 17:8

Babylon the Great is the forerunner to the Antichrist. Satan will use the great city to prepare the world to worship his Antichrist. The Antichrist will only allow the global influence of the great city of Babylon to continue for as long as it serves his purpose. He will wait until the inhabitants of earth are fully drunk with the spirituality of Babylon before making his move. The people of earth must become

---

[15] 2 Thes. 2:4.

so spiritually inebriated and morally spineless that they will be quickly dominated by his tyranny. Once the spirituality of Babylon intoxicates the earth with spiritual delusion and robs it of conviction, the time will be ripe for the Antichrist's reign. The Bible tells us that the nations, drunk with the confusion of Babylon, will willingly invite the leadership of the Antichrist. All of Babylon's freedoms will be quickly displaced by totalitarianism of the highest order. Those who have refused to be fascinated by the glory of God and have instead chosen to be fascinated by the harlot will ultimately be enthralled by the Antichrist.

SIXTEEN
THE ELIJAH GENERATION

*Behold, I will send you Elijah the prophet before
the great and awesome day of the Lord comes.*
—Malachi 4:5

God gives mandates to entire generations. He called
Moses' generation out of Egyptian bondage to walk
through the wilderness in obedience. He called Joshua's
generation to take the land promised to Abraham. He
called the generation of Zerubbabel to rebuild the temple
in Jerusalem. We are also a chosen generation. God has
also called us to a specific task in the end times. The final
generation of this age carries a unique mandate to be forerunners who prepare the way for the return of Lord.[1]

The Bible promises that before the day of the Lord
comes, the prophet Elijah will be sent. We know that this
prophecy pointed to John the Baptist as the Elijah of his
generation (Mt. 11:14, 17:12). We also know that this
prophecy will have a dynamic fulfillment in Jerusalem in

---

[1] Certainly all Christians of every generation share certain universal
mandates, such as to love God and disciple all nations. But the
Church in the end times will have a unique calling to prepare the way
of the Lord.

the end times.[2] The book of Revelation makes it clear that while the land of Israel will be the most intense focal point of end-time activity, the entire earth will experience similar events. In other words, the events taking place in Israel will be experienced around the world to a lesser degree, as God brings history to a climax at the second coming of His Son.

While the coming of Elijah will have its most dynamic fulfillment in Jerusalem through the two witnesses, the promise will also have a global expression through the end-time Church. Like He did with John the Baptist, God will empower end-time forerunners, the final generation of this age, to call the nations to repentance and announce the second coming. We will prepare the way of the Lord by calling for repentance and faith in the name of the soon-coming Lord Jesus.

While many in the Church still insist on teaching that believers can expect to be secretly raptured before the events of the end times begin, that conviction cannot be sustained either biblically or theologically.[3] Throughout the entire history of the Church, Christians have faced intense persecution and have laid down their lives for the sake of the gospel. Even today Christians around the world are imprisoned, beaten, and murdered for loving Jesus. Yet somehow much of the church in America has bought into a preposterous notion that all Christians will go to heaven before the promised days of adversity come.

---

[2] Revelation 11:3–13 gives an account of how, in the midst of world-wide judgments, the Lord will raise up two witnesses in Jerusalem who will operate in the same kind of power as Elijah did during his ministry.

[3] "The theological and exegetical grounds for pretribulationism rest on insufficient evidence, non sequitur reasoning, and faulty exegesis." Gundry, *The Church and the Tribulation*, 10.

Believers have a crucial role in the end times. The final generation of Christians will be a generation of forerunners. Just as John the Baptist proclaimed the coming of the Lord and prepared his generation for the Messiah, so the last generation will carry this same mandate before God. Like John, the last generation will come in the spirit and power of the prophet Elijah (Lk. 1:17). The prophetic anointing of Elijah will powerfully propel the Church forward in fulfilling our destiny. What God did through John the Baptist to announce the first coming of His Son, He will do through us as an Elijah generation to announce His second coming.

If we truly are forerunners called to be an Elijah generation, then we ought to take a closer look at one of the Old Testament's greatest prophets to see what it means to be called to minister in the spirit and power of Elijah. As we examine what the Bible teaches about the time of Elijah, we will discover striking parallels between Elijah's ministry and the end-time mission of the Church. In fact, the days of Elijah seem to give us a prophetic picture of the end times. Elijah and Jezebel were individuals who foreshadowed the end-time showdown between the Elijah generation and the great harlot.

The Days of Elijah

Elijah lived in the most perilous period of Israel's history. It was a time of great upheaval as the Lord disciplined His wayward people. God struck the land with a three-and-a-half-year drought that brought severe famine.[4] There was unprecedented persecution against men

---

[4] Jesus identifies that the drought of Elijah lasted three and a half years in Luke 4:25. This is the same period of time that the two witnesses will prophesy in the end times (Rev. 11:3).

of God as a sinister campaign was waged to terminate every true prophet in the nation (1 Kgs. 18:13–14). Israel was overrun with idolatrous practices and pagan clerics. The widespread worship of Baal introduced licentious observances that included religious prostitution.[5] Four hundred false prophets of the pagan god Asherah were dining in the royal court (1 Kgs. 18:19). Nearly the entire population of Israel had bowed the knee to Baal.[6] Injustice and murder characterized the political leadership (1 Kgs. 19:18). The days of Elijah's ministry were the most dire the nation of Israel had ever faced.

> There was none who sold himself to do what was evil in the sight of the LORD like Ahab, whom Jezebel his wife incited.
>
> —1 Kings 21:25

The greatest evils of those days sprang from a single source. The pagan wave that washed over the entire nation and nearly eliminated every representative of the Lord was due to the influence of the most infamous woman of the Bible, Jezebel. This one woman led the entire nation of Israel into apostasy. She was the queen who sat upon the throne of Israel and was renowned for her whoring and sorcery (2 Kgs. 9:22). She seduced the king of Israel away from the Lord and lured him to worship her demon gods. Under the powerful influence of Jezebel, the king became apostate; he completely fell away from the God of his fathers. It was written of Ahab that he did more evil and more to provoke the Lord to wrath than anyone before him had done (1 Kgs. 16:30, 33).

---

5   Wood, *The Prophets of Israel*, 210.

6   The Lord had only reserved 7,000 Israelites for Himself, a small fraction of Israel's population.

Apostasy and Persecution

This ancient biblical account is a striking foreshadowing of the scenario that will play out in the end times as the Elijah generation faces off with the Babylon generation. Elijah fulfilled his calling in the context of apostasy in the land of Israel. The Church in the end times will also face a time when Babylon will lead the world into apostasy. Leaders from all religious affiliations will come together in an effort to unify the nations. Jews, Christians, moderate Muslims, Hindus, and Buddhists will agree to link arms under one syncretistic banner. This movement will look like the answer the world has been waiting for. With great fanfare, the people of earth will celebrate this triumph. Like Ahab, many "Christian" leaders will follow the harlot's lead and tout this new religion as being what Jesus would want for His Church and the world. The unifying of the world religions will be considered a marvelous victory. The highest priority of this movement will be human good and human glory. All conviction about the true God will melt away to nothing.

Like Elijah, the Church will face a time when many will be offended and fall away.[7] The prophesied apostasy will be one of the most difficult hours in the history of the Church. The Lord forewarned us of the great falling away because the tragic intensity of the end-time apostasy will seem unbearable. Elijah was haunted by the fact that so many of his countrymen had bowed their knees to Baal. He repeatedly spoke of himself as the only remaining prophet in Israel (1 Kgs. 18:22, 19:14). Israel's apostasy wore heavy on the prophet's heart.

One of the clearest characteristics of Elijah's ministry

[7] "Let no man deceive you by any means: for that day shall not come, except there come a falling away first" (2 Thes. 2:3, KJV).

was that of confrontation. Whether in the face of the apostate king of Israel or the false prophets of Baal, Elijah refused to back down from a God-ordained fight. Even when he was outnumbered 450 to one, Elijah stood confident in the power of God. On one occasion, when King Ahab saw Elijah, he said to him, "Is it you, you troubler of Israel?" In classic form, Elijah answered the most politically powerful man in Israel with a strong retort: "I have not troubled Israel, but you have, and your father's house, because you have abandoned the commandments of the Lord and followed the Baals" (1 Kgs. 18:17–18). Elijah never shrank from proclaiming the truth in the face of compromise, no matter the circumstances.

The end-time church will be maligned and intensely resisted when the false religion of Babylon the Great dominates the world. This assault will find its fiercest expression through the ones who are most deeply compromised with Babylon. In Elijah's day, it was Ahab. In Jesus' day, it was the chief priests. And in the end times, it is nearly certain that the leaders of the apostate church will bring the greatest persecution to the faithful. But the end-time church will not shrink from this confrontation. Just as Elijah would not shy away from speaking the truth to Ahab, the forerunners will faithfully proclaim the truth to those who have compromised with the spirit of Babylon and aligned themselves with the kingdom of darkness.

In Elijah's day it was illegal to be a man of God. Jezebel had marked every prophet of the Lord for death. As one who stood true to the Lord, Elijah was a marked man. He alone would not bend his knee before the harlot's influence, and there was no one more hated in the apostate royal court. Like Jezebel, the great harlot, Babylon, will criminalize those who stand true to the Lord.

Just as Jezebel made a concerted effort to rid Israel of every prophet of the Lord, in the end times Babylon the Great will become drunk with the blood of Christian martyrs. The forerunner generation will be perceived as Babylon's greatest threat. The Church in the end times will be given supernatural grace to withstand the pressures of persecution of Babylon. While not every believer will be martyred, many will. Throughout Church history, those who are elected to martyrdom are given the grace they need to glorify the Father in the hour of death. The Elijah generation will overcome Babylon, confident in the certainty of resurrection!

Releasing Judgment

Part of the calling to walk in the spirit and power of Elijah includes partnering with God as He releases His judgments. God used Elijah in a special prophetic role in the nation when He put him in charge of when and if it would rain. Elijah partnered with God in a three-and-a-half-year famine that touched all of Israel. God not only answered Elijah's prayer to bring the drought, but He also put it in his power to make it rain (Jas. 5:17; 1 Kgs. 17:1).

During the years of drought and famine, Elijah never gave in to the human need for rain. The severe famine came upon Israel because the nation had fallen away from her God in favor of false religion. Elijah would not compromise his partnership with the Lord's judgment in order to relieve widespread human suffering. Nor would he pray for the drought to end because of the pressure of persecution. King Ahab blamed Elijah for Israel's trouble, though Ahab's compromised leadership was the true reason for the famine. The judgment would not be lifted until Israel repented. As Elijah partnered with God in His discipline of

Israel, he managed to maintain an eternal perspective.

The end-time church will be partnering with God through intercession as He releases disaster upon cities and nations around the world. Believers living in the end times will need to maintain an eternal perspective while interceding with God during the release of His judgments on earth. God's wrath is terrifying. Because He is so utterly holy, His anger toward sin is an insatiable inferno that is difficult for us to understand. Great human suffering will undoubtedly result from God's end-time judgments. While this suffering will be beyond our human comprehension, we will need to be grounded in the truth that God is working in the least severe way to bring the greatest number of people to repentance and faith in His Son. As we partner with God in sending drought and famine to the earth, we will be pressured by human need and the threat of persecution because of our stand. Those deceived by the spirit of Babylon will believe that the Church is the greatest threat to human survival because we are asking God to continue to press the nations with calamity. But if God will not yield until repentance occurs, then neither can we.

Love Is the Law

While our generation will certainly be equipped in the spirit and power of Elijah, we must always remember the loving aim of our Lord. When Jesus sent messengers to a Samaritan village in order to prepare it for His arrival, the Samaritans rejected the messengers and would not allow Jesus to stay with them. When the messengers returned to Jesus with news of the rejection, James and John said to Him,

"Lord, do you want us to tell fire to come down from heaven and consume them as Elijah did?" But He turned and rebuked them and said, "You do not know what manner of spirit you are of; for the Son of Man came not to destroy people's lives but to save them."

—Luke 9:54–55

While Elijah would not compromise His partnership with God for human interest, that reality never contradicted ministering mercy to the needy. Elijah was not only a vessel of God's judgment; he was also a vessel of God's mercy. He was sent to a poor widow and her son in the days of the famine. The woman had come to the end of her food supply and expected that starvation would soon end their lives. In response to her utter desperation, Elijah did a miracle that would supernaturally multiply her supply of flour and sustain the lives of her and her son until the famine ended. While we know that God takes no pleasure in the destruction of the wicked, we also know that He takes great pleasure in coming to help the widow and the orphan.[8] Whether Elijah was releasing drought and famine or was supernaturally providing food for starving widows, he lived in constant partnership with God.

As the Elijah generation, we must live in the love of God and ever align our hearts with the merciful and life-saving agenda of the Lord. The coming judgments in the end times have one purpose: to bring the earth to repentance before the return of Jesus. An eternity in hell is at stake for every individual on earth. God will release wars, famines, earthquakes, and pestilence, bringing tremendous suffering in this age in order to steer souls away from

---

[8]   Ezek. 18:23; Jas. 1:27.

unending suffering in the next. Still, many casualties will result from the coming wars and disasters. Drought and famine will severely afflict many parts of the earth. Food shortages will be common. In the midst of this affliction, the Church will arise and be empowered to testify of Jesus with signs and wonders. Many have cried out for the spirit and power of Elijah. God promises that we shall have it. But we shall have it in the same context that Elijah did: apostasy and judgment. Like Elijah, the end-time Church will be supernaturally empowered to minister mercy to the needy. Jesus will once again multiply fish and bread for the poor and desperate masses, but this time He will do it through His Church in His final campaign to win hearts and show forth His glory.

The Fall of Babylon

> And of Jezebel the LORD also said, "The dogs
> shall eat Jezebel within the walls of Jezreel."
> —1 Kings 21:23

Elijah's calling to confront the apostasy of his day climaxed in the proclamation of Jezebel's fall. Only one person was more powerful than the apostate king of Israel. Though Ahab was the political figurehead of the nation, Jezebel was the true fountainhead. She was the one who controlled the political direction of the nation. She had all of Israel at her disposal, and still the mighty prophet would not shrink back from proclaiming her demise. Imagine her indignation when she heard Elijah's prophecy that dogs would eat her dead body within the city. It is difficult to imagine a more politically incorrect prophecy given to a more powerful and corrupt woman. With fearless confidence in the Lord, Elijah declared that the most powerful woman in Israel would become dog chow.

Just as Elijah foretold the fall of Jezebel, God will em-power the Church in the end times to proclaim the fall of Babylon the Great. It will seem like the prosperity of Baby-lon will never end; it will seem as if the city is invincible. Yet in the midst of Babylon's growing power and influence, the Church will faithfully proclaim its ultimate demise. When the Church discerns the wicked power at work behind the great city and proclaims its inevitable fall, it will certainly not be a popular message among the citizenry of Baby-lon. As sin abounds in the world, God's grace will abound all the more in the Church. Through Spirit-empowered prayer and preaching, the Church will overcome the spirit of Babylon. Just as the propagation of sin will lead to un-precedented demonic activity in the earth, God will use the day and night intercession of the Church to truly open the heavens and pour His power down. This end-time revival will make the great harlot even more furious. The spirit of Babylon will so confuse and control the nations through lust that they will persecute the Church in greater measure as God empowers the Church to resist and proclaim the great harlot's fall.

> And you shall strike down the house of Ahab
> your master, so that I may avenge on Jezebel
> the blood of my servants the prophets, and the
> blood of all the servants of the Lord.
>   —2 Kings 9:7

Elijah was not on earth long enough to see his proph-ecy against Jezebel fulfilled. But nothing could stop the Word of God from coming to pass. Jezebel had not only led the entire nation of Israel into apostasy, her hands were still stained with the blood of God's friends, the prophets. While in all likelihood she had forgotten about the orders she had given to kill the servants of God, God had not forgotten even one of those servants who were slain. Jezebel's sins had reached heaven and there was only one thing left for her.

Sudden and Unforeseen

She never saw her fall coming. An Israelite military commander by the name of Jehu was riding into her city, fully intending to take the throne from her. When she received the news that this *coup d'etat* had arisen, she knew exactly what action she would take. She would do what she always did—use her seductive powers to conquer Jehu. Like a seductress trying to capture the lust of men with her image, she painted her eyes and adorned her head. She sat in an exalted position and looked out of the window.

As Jehu rode into the city and passed through the gate, he saw her peering out of the window at him. Jezebel quickly tried to exercise the feminine influence that had dominated many other politically ambitious men. She aggressively accused Jehu of treachery and murder, confident that he would see her beauty and realize the error of his deeds. But for the first time, Jezebel's beauty and deception would not prevail, for Jehu was a man anointed and commissioned by God for this task.

Jehu called to any who would join his insurrection. Only Jezebel's eunuchs had the courage to seize her. She never expected that her own personal assistants would be the ones to throw her out of the window. In a single moment, the seductive beauty that had lured all of Israel away from Yahweh splattered upon the ground. Before any plans were made for her burial, the town dogs had already picked her bones clean.

> Then a mighty angel took up a stone like a great millstone and threw it into the sea, saying, "So will Babylon the great city be thrown down with violence, and will be found no more . . . And in her was found the blood of prophets and of saints, and of all who have been slain on earth."
>
> —Revelation 18:21, 24

Just as swiftly and thoroughly as Jezebel was thrown down, Babylon the Great will meet her end. When God comes to the last of His end-time judgments, He will remember to make Babylon the Great drink the final dregs of His fury (Rev. 16:19). The plagues that God will unleash upon the great city will come suddenly. The greatest earthquake in history will rock the earth and every city will be toppled (Rev. 16:18–19). But no city will fall farther and harder than Babylon the Great. In a moment, the city that once knew only pleasure, luxury, and decadence will be tormented with death, mourning, and famine. In a single day, that invincible city will be thrown down with violence and utterly burned. The moment that the Elijah generation has been proclaiming in spite of severe persecution will finally come.

When Babylon the Great is destroyed, her fall will be swift and complete; it will be in the pomp and pride of her seemingly invincible position. The inhabitants will not see it coming. At the height of wealth and prosperity, she will crash. Unlike Rome and ancient Babylon, God's judgment of the great harlot will not be a slow demise; it will be sudden and complete destruction. Her sudden fall will shock the earth, and all those who loved the great city will be horrified at the strength of God's wrath against her.

The political leaders of the nations who had gained their power by compromising with the power of Babylon will weep and wail over the city's destruction (Rev. 18:19). The businessmen will mourn when they see the city burn, because they know that the days of profiting from her commerce are over (Rev. 18:11). The tears shed for Babylon will not be for the sake of the city itself; the weeping will be because her lurid pleasures will never again be tasted. All the nations that had become rich, that had satisfied every desire through their affiliation with the great harlot, will lament when the city falls.

But to heaven and to all who love the truth, the fall of Babylon will be God's vindication of His saints. While the earth is bewailing the sight of her burning, heaven will be rejoicing, celebrating the righteous judgment of God. Angels and saints will sing of God's justice and might. The day of Babylon's fall will be a day justice prevails. All who love the truth shall glory in God's judgment of the harlot.

Never to Rise Again

Once God has used the great city of Babylon to sift the nations, the only purpose He will have left for her is to demonstrate His wrath. The city that had luxuriously exalted itself to the heavens will be utterly destroyed. Not a single one of the magnificent sky-scraping structures of Babylon will pierce heaven. Never once will the God of heaven sit up and admire the accomplishments of fallen humans. Instead, the sins of the great city will have been laid brick by brick until they reached into the court of heaven and demanded divine judgment. Though the inhabitants of Babylon the Great will not realize it, day-by-day their blasphemously ignorant efforts will be written in a book. Every act of pride and lust will be recorded in heaven. The days will become months and the months may turn to decades. But when the cup of sin begins to overflow, when the justice of God cannot bear to allow another sin, God will make known to the nations that the Mighty One alone is the judge of the earth.

> Rejoice over her, O heaven, and you saints and apostles and prophets, for God has given judgment for you against her!
> —Revelation 18:20

The judgment of Babylon will not be for her sorcery and immorality alone. The primary reason that Babylon the Great will suffer so severely will be the way she persecuted the Church in the end times. God will not allow the murder of His servants to go unavenged. Babylon's judgment will be evidence that the courtroom of heaven has ruled in favor of the saints. Just as Jezebel was eaten by dogs for the righteous blood she shed, Babylon the Great will be devastated for the murderous treatment of God's holy ones.

After Babylon the Great falls, no form of Babylon will ever rise again. To illustrate this point, in Revelation 18 the angel takes up a great millstone and throws it into the sea. The imagery of a stone throne into the sea is repeatedly used for Babylon's final fall. Jeremiah used it (Jer. 51:63), and the Lord Jesus used it in connection with those who cause His people to stumble (Mt. 18:6). Babylon will be the greatest force to ever cause God's people to stumble. Because of this, the great harlot will be thrown down with violence. This prophetic declaration of a sudden fall without recovery could not have been meant for either ancient Babylon or Rome. Only the fall of the eschatological city of Babylon the Great can fulfill such an unmistakable prophecy. Like a millstone thrown into the ocean, Babylon will fall and never rise again.

SEVENTEEN

BABYLON AND BEYOND

SINCE THE FLOOD, fallen humans have sought after a civilization free from their Creator, utilizing every one of their God-given abilities to build a city and tower that would reach into heaven. Lured by the promise of pleasure and progress, fallen humans have followed the leadership of an ancient demonic principality. The harlot spirit of Babylon has repeatedly inspired her clientele with dreams of a new age and a golden civilization. Fallen humans have all too eagerly joined themselves with the harlot's agenda and adopted her ideologies—religious syncretism and moral relativism.

Since the glory of first-century Rome, no other city has risen to the same level of power and glory in the earth. Although the harlot power lost her throne, she did not lose her influence. Since then, the spirit of Babylon has been active behind the scenes, spreading her influence throughout the world. In our day the harlot power has begun growing to new heights, her seductions gaining ground in human affairs. Postmodernism, the sexual revolution, the social continuum toward religious syncretism, and the embrace of every form of immorality are all clear evidence that the spirit of Babylon is ascending in power. Her ancient influence is uniting the world in a campaign to ready the nations for her final expression.

As the generation that will see the end of the age, we are now on the brink of the greatest manifestation of Babylon in history. While we don't know how many years we have left, the Bible declares several cataclysmic events that will come before the Lord returns. Among them is the rise of Babylon the Great. This city will be the greatest expression of the harlot spirit in history. The power and influence of Babel, Babylon, and Rome at their respective zeniths all foreshadowed the political scope and cultural sway this eschatological city will carry in the end times. In her rise, Genesis 11 will be repeated. The nations will come together, unified in language and purpose to make for themselves a name with no regard for their Creator God. And it will seem as if nothing that they imagine will be impossible for them.

Babylon the Great is the demonic counterpart to the New Jerusalem. In every way, Satan's final city will epitomize diametric opposition to God's eternal city. The New Jerusalem is the Bride prepared for Christ, the Son of God. Babylon the Great is a harlot exploited for the purposes of the Antichrist, the son of perdition. The New Jerusalem comes from God out of heaven and is the dwelling for all who live in agreement with God, both the Jew and the Gentile. Babylon the Great arises from men living in agreement with demons. Christ will cherish and preserve His Bride forever. The Antichrist will turn on the harlot and burn the city with fire. The New Jerusalem is the holy city. Babylon the Great fills up the full measure of sin. The New Jerusalem is eternal. Babylon's judgment will come in an hour and her destruction will be total; she will never rise again.

Though the biblical reality of Babylon the Great is horrifying, we know that the promises and seductions of the harlot will appear very differently in the sight of men. To those who walk in the truth, Babylon the Great is a repulsive harlot spreading filth throughout the earth. But to those in league with the harlot and drunk with her wine, Babylon the Great will appear as mankind's last and best hope. The harlot will be robed in the most glorious apparel and adorned in the most coveted jewels. Every man will want to be with her and every woman will want to be her. This city will capture the imagination of every political, religious, and business leader in the world. By all accounts, Babylon the Great will be hailed as the most spectacular of all human accomplishments. Its architecture, political infrastructure, commercial power, cultural influence, and religious innovations will inspire the world. The promises of the harlot spirit will seduce mankind once more. But this final manifestation of Babylon, though by far her greatest, will be her last.

Where Will Babylon Be Located?

How and where this city will arise is not clearly shown to us in biblical prophecy. Questions like, "What will lead to the building of Babylon the Great?" and "Where will the geographical location of Babylon the Great be?" while legitimate and intriguing, elude our power to answer. We can only continue to ponder until the actual events occur. Some believe that Rome will once again rise as the capital of a neo-Roman Empire. Others believe that the harlot city will be built on the ancient site of the original Babylon in Iraq. But, as we have seen, the spirit of Babylon is not limited geographically. There are good reasons to believe that it could be either location, but the fact remains that we simply cannot be sure.

It may seem that a city of this magnitude will not be built anytime soon, but a project like this may not take as long as we think. If all the nations determine to build a city and direct the world's resources toward the objective, as was done in Genesis 11, constructing the metropolis will not take long. Berlin was only a few short years away from becoming the world's capital, had the technology for the atomic bomb been discovered first by Nazi scientists. Just one twist of fate would have radically changed world history. There is no telling just how quickly world events can unfold when our sovereign God begins to call them forth.

Even today, there is an intriguing example of a city that is becoming a global center almost overnight. The United Arab Emirates is quickly becoming the envy of the world, and a collaborative international effort has made Dubai the fastest growing city on earth. The plans are staggering. When finished, its business district will feature 500 skyscrapers. Its waterfront will be two and a half times the length of Washington DC's and seven times that of Manhattan Island. The world's tallest building is scheduled to be finished in the coming years. This tower, which will reach further into the heavens than any other man-made structure, is called the Burj Dubai.[1] The only structure scheduled to compete with the record-breaking height of the Burj Dubai is the Al Burj, another tower planned for the city of Dubai. The low-wage labor imported to construct the endless building projects is considered by many to be

[1] The vision of the Burj Dubai promises an "unprecedented example of international cooperation—a symbol—a beacon of progress for the entire world." Emaar Properties PJSC, "Vision."

nothing less than slavery. World-famous musicians and actors are purchasing property there. The greatest architects and businessmen from around the world are fully intent on making Dubai the greatest city in the world.

Could Dubai be the place of the harlot's greatest expression? We simply don't yet know. If so, several events must lead to Dubai becoming the political, religious, and economic capital of the world. If not, it is at least a stunning example of just how quickly a city of this magnitude can take shape.

The City of God

Babylon the Great promises to be a spectacle, but no matter how amazingly fascinating Babylon turns out to be in the eyes of the nations, the people of God will remain strangers to it. The harlot will seduce the world with her promise of human progress and achievement, but God's people will ever be aliens, aware of her dark agenda as a forerunner to the Antichrist. We are strangers in Babylon, and as long as we bear the Spirit of Christ, we will continue to be, until God forever makes an end of her. We are looking to another city in another country. The longing in our hearts can be satisfied by one thing alone. Our citizenship is a heavenly one; we have been fashioned for the celestial city.

> In my Father's house are many rooms. If it were not so, would I have told you that I go to prepare a place for you? And if I go and prepare a place for you, I will come again and will take you to myself, that where I am you may be also.
> —John 14:2–3

Strangers in Babylon cannot escape the feeling that there is something missing in this life. We fight to carry our hearts before God, believing in what He has promised. But much of what God has placed in us will not be fulfilled in this age, for this is the age of Babylon. We live in the culture and are surrounded by the priorities of Babylon, the beauty and promises of the world vying to capture our imaginations. Yet like Zerubbabel, we live as foreigners and aliens within our current circumstances. Something deep within eats at us; it's a groaning for another order, a longing for another city. We simply cannot be satisfied with anything that is destined to fall; we have been stamped with eternity. Once we have turned our backs on sin and our confederation with Satan's rebellion, the Lord marks us. We live with an imprint of the Son of God on our hearts, and will never be satisfied until we see Him face to face. Our home is our Savior. The longing in our hearts that make us strangers in Babylon points us to our true citizenship in the New Jerusalem.

The day is coming when all sin will be finished. The earth will begin a new age under the direct rule of a new, Jewish king of a new city. The days of pursuing a civilization without the Creator will come to an end as the Creator comes to reclaim His creation. The Righteous One will split the sky and every eye will see Deity in the form of a Jewish man accompanied by the full glory of heaven. Just when it seems that darkness has overcome the world and the demonic agenda for the earth has prevailed, a light will break through. Jesus will come to His Bride.

The cry of the ages will finally be answered. Our longings will ultimately be satisfied. We will no longer be strangers but citizens. The groaning of all creation under the weight of sin will end at the sight of our King. God will answer the desire He instilled in us that made us look beyond Babylon and the trappings of this age; He will answer with His Son's return to the earth. When we see Him, when He looks into our eyes, we will be home.

WORKS CITED AND RECOMMENDED REFERENCES

Baldwin, Joyce G. *Tyndale Old Testament Commentaries: Haggai, Zechariah, Malachi.* Downers Grove: InterVarsity Press, 1972.

Banks, Aaron. "ONE Sabbath: Live Your Beliefs," *One.org.* http://www.one.org/blog/2007/10/05/one-sabboth-live-your-beliefs.

Bickle, Mike. *The Pleasures of Loving God.* Lake Mary, Florida: Creation House, 2000.

Boyd, Gregory A. *God at War: The Bible and Spiritual Conflict.* Downers Grove: InterVarsity Press, 1997.

Champlin, Edward. *Nero.* Cambridge: Harvard University Press, 2003.

Dante. *The Portable Dante.* Translated by Mark Musa. New York: Penguin Books, 1995.

Diodorus Siculus. *Book II.* Translated by Charles H. Oldfather. Cambridge: Harvard University Press, 1933.

Douglass, Steve. "Endorsements." Call2All.org. http://call2all.org/Articles/1000043153/Call2All/Contact_Us/

Press_Room/Endorsements/Steve_Douglass_President.aspx.

Driver, Samuel R. *The Book of Daniel*. London: Cambridge University Press, 1922.

Dunn, James D. G. *The Theology of Paul the Apostle.* Grand Rapids: Eerdmans, 1998.

Friedman, Thomas L. *The World is Flat: A Brief History of the Twenty-first Century*. FSG Books: New York, 2005.

Gundry, Robert H. *The Church and the Tribulation: A Biblical Examination of Posttribulationism.* Grand Rapids: Zondervan, 1973.

Henry, Patrick. *Liberty Tree.ca.* http://quotes.liberty-tree.ca/quotes_by/patrick+henry.

Herodotus. *The Histories, Book I*. Translated by George C. Macaulay. Introduction and notes by Donald Lateiner. New York: Barnes and Noble, 2004.

Hitchcock, Roswell D. *Hitchcock's Bible Names Dictionary.* Christian Classics Ethereal Library. S.v. "Zerubbabel." http://www.ccel.org/ccel/hitchcock/bible_names.html?term=zerubbabel.

Horsley, Richard A., ed. *Paul and Empire: Religion and Power in Roman Imperial Society.* Trinity Press: Harrisburg, PA, 1997.

Josephus. *Josephus: The Complete Works.* Translated by William Whiston. Nashville: Thomas Nelson Publishers, 1998.

Ladd, George E. *A Commentary on the Revelation of John.* Grand Rapids: Eerdmans, 1972.

Marshall, I. Howard, A. R. Millard, J. I. Packer, and D. J. Wiseman. *New Bible Dictionary.* Downers Grove: Inter-Varsity Press, 1996.

Mathews, Kenneth A. *The New American Commentary: Genesis 1–11:26.* Nashville: Broadman & Holman Publishers, 1994.

McDonough-Taub, Gloria. "Porn at Work: Recognizing A Sex Addict." CNBC.com. http://www.cnbc.com/id/31922685/site/14081545.

Mead, Walter Russell. *Special Providence: American Foreign Policy and How It Changed the World.* New York: Routledge, 2002.

Miller, Joshua R. "Fusion Centers Expand Criteria to Identify Militia Members." FOXNews.com. http://www.foxnews.com/politics/first100days/2009/03/23/fusion-centers-expand-criteria-identify-militia-members.

Miller, Stephen R. *The New American Commentary: Daniel.* Nashville: Broadman & Holman Publishers, 1994.

Mounce, Robert H. *The New International Commentary on the New Testament: The Book of Revelation.* Grand Rapids: Eerdmans Publishing Company, 1998.

Murray, Andrew. "Fifth Lesson." *With Christ in the School of Prayer.* http://prayerfoundation.org/booktexts/z_andrew_murray_schoolofprayer_15.htm.

Oates, John. *Babylon.* London: Thames and Hudson, 1986.

Pink, Arthur W. *The Antichrist: A Systematic Study of Satan's Counterfeit Christ.* Grand Rapids: Kregel, 1988.

Piper, John. *The Pleasures of God.* Sisters, Oregon: Multnomah Publishers, 2000.

Plato. *The Portable Plato.* Translated by Scott Buchanan. New York: Penguin Books, 1977.

Roux, Georges. *Ancient Iraq.* London: Penguin Books, 1992.

Sproul, Robert C. *The Last Days According to Jesus.* Grand Rapids: Baker Books, 1998.

St. Augustine. *The City of God.* New York: Barnes and Noble, 2006.

Tacitus. *The Annals of Imperial Rome.* Translated by Michael Grant. London: Penguin Books, 1996.

Taha, Abir. *Nietzsche, Prophet of Nazism: The Cult of the Superman*. Bloomington, IN: Author House, 2005.

Thomas, Robert L. *Revelation 8–22: An Exegetical Commentary.* Chicago: Moody Press, 1995.

Tolle, Eckhart. *The Power of Now: A Guide to Spiritual Enlightment*. Novato: New World Library, 1996.

Walvoord, John F. *The Revelation of Jesus Christ.* Chicago: Moody Press, 1966.

Wiseman, Donald J. *Nebuchadrezzar [sic] and Babylon.* Oxford, UK: Oxford University Press, 1983.

Wistrich, Robert S. *Hitler and the Holocaust.* New York: Random House, 2003.

Wood, Leon J. *The Prophets of Israel.* Grand Rapids: Baker Books, 1979.

World Council of Religious Leaders. "About the World Council of Religious Leaders." http://www.millennium-peacesummit.com.

Exodus Cry
The Prayer Movement to End Slavery

AT LEAST 27 million people are currently enslaved around the globe. 75% of them are enslaved for sexual exploitation. Another person is bought or sold every 8 seconds. And every 30 seconds, that victim is a child.

EACH YEAR over 600,000 people are trafficked across international borders for the purpose of sexual exploitation. 80% of these are female. 50% are children.

NEARLY EVERY COUNTRY on the face of the earth is involved in the global sex trade both as a source and a destination for women and children—this includes America.

WOMEN AND CHILDREN trafficked for sexual exploitation generate tens of billions of dollars every year. Human trafficking is the fastest growing criminal enterprise on the earth.

THE PRICE of a slave in 1850 (by today's currency) was $40,000. Today, the average purchase price of a slave is $90.

International House of Prayer
Missions Base of Kansas City

....

24/7 Live Worship and Prayer
IHOP.org

....

Since September 19, 1999, we have continued in night and day prayer with worship as the foundation of our ministry to win the lost, heal the sick, and make disciples as we labor alongside the larger Body of Christ to see the Great Commission fulfilled and to function as forerunners who prepare the way for the return of Jesus. By the grace of God, we are committed to combining 24/7 prayers for justice with 24/7 works for justice until the Lord returns. We do this best as our lives are rooted in prayer that focuses on intimacy with God and intercession for breakthrough of the fullness of God's power and purpose for this generation.

For more information on our internships, conferences, university, live prayer room webcast, and more, please visit our website at IHOP.org.

International House of Prayer Missions Base
3535 E. Red Bridge Road, Kansas City, MO 64137
816.763.0200 • info@ihop.org • IHOP.org

IHOPU

International House of Prayer University

Ministry, Music, Media, and eSchool
IHOP.org/university

International House of Prayer University (IHOPU) is a full-time Bible school which exists to equip this generation in the knowledge of God and the power of the Spirit for the bold proclamation of the Lord Jesus and His return.

Students embrace rigorous theological training and Sermon on the Mount lifestyles in the context of a thriving missions base fueled by night and day prayer (IHOP–KC). As a result, theological education obtained in the classroom is intrinsically connected to intimacy with Jesus and hands-on experience. IHOPU is led by qualified leaders of the missions base.

IHOPU is distinct from many other institutions of higher learning in the United States in that we seek a holistic approach to education with an emphasis on the forerunner ministry, and a NightWatch training element.

International House of Prayer University
3535 E. Red Bridge Road, Kansas City, MO 64137
816.763.0243 • ihopu@ihop.org • IHOP.org/university

BOOK OF REVELATION STUDY GUIDE
with notes by Mike Bickle

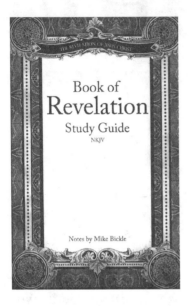

A simple but inspiring, verse-by-verse guide to the book of Revelation, with a glossary of terms and symbols, and in-depth articles and charts. Mike Bickle's straightforward approach brings the message to life and emphasizes its relevance for us today.

Gain understanding of some of Mike's most compelling insights into the book of Revelation:

- As an "end-time Book of Acts," it reveals God's glorious plan to use a lovesick Bride at the end of the age in unprecedented power and authority. She will partner with Jesus as He cleanses our planet of evil and ushers in the kingdom of God.

- It's an "infallible prayer manual" that maps out the global, strategic prayers of the praying church. We'll be equipped to pray in unity with Jesus' heart as He unleashes His judgments upon the Antichrist's evil empire.

- While many saints are waiting to "go up" in the rapture to avoid the tribulation, God is waiting for the church to "grow up" to release the tribulation judgments by prayer on the Antichrist. This is truly the Church's greatest hour.

This book is a must-read!